Mary E. (Mary Ellen) Bamford

TI:

A Story of San Francisco's Chinatown

Mary E. (Mary Ellen) Bamford

TI:
A Story of San Francisco's Chinatown

ISBN/EAN: 9783744669757

Printed in Europe, USA, Canada, Australia, Japan

Cover: Foto ©Thomas Meinert / pixelio.de

More available books at **www.hansebooks.com**

TI:

A STORY OF SAN FRANCISCO'S CHINATOWN.

By MARY E. BAMFORD.

CHICAGO:
DAVID C. COOK PUBLISHING COMPANY,
36 WASHINGTON STREET.

TI:
A STORY OF SAN FRANCISCO'S CHINATOWN.

CHAPTER I.

THE "NEW WORDS."

IT WAS low tide. Ti sat on a board at the end of the net-drying platform, and looked out beyond the mud flats of the bay. He could see his father's junk far on the water. The junk had

TI.

been away down the bay to San Francisco, and now was coming back, bringing a load of salt to be used in curing shrimps. Thousands of shrimps were caught and dried every year at this isolated California Chinese fishing-village where Ti lived. There were large plank floors on which the shrimps were dried. Tons of shrimps were shipped across the ocean to China yearly.

His uncle, Lum Lee, hurried past to get some wood to be used as fuel in some of the processes of curing shrimps. As he ran by, he looked at Ti and observed that if the boy should fall off the board at the end of the net-drying platform, he would land in the mud-flat underneath.

"Do not fall," he called out in Chinese, as he ran.

But Ti felt entirely above such advice. Of course he could hold on! But what he could not do was to hurry the coming in of the tide, so that his father could bring the junk to the wharf. Ti particularly wanted the junk to hurry, because, when going away, his father had said that he would bring something from the great city for a present to his boy. And now, when the junk was returning and fairly in sight of the fishing-camp, the water near the shore line of the bay must go out and leave nothing but mud-flats! What junk could sail on a mud-flat? Ti did wish that the water would hurry coming in, so he could get his present!

What would it be? Would it be a toy

balloon, such as the American children had sometimes? Or would it be some rice cakes? Perhaps it would be a fish-bladder covered with feathers, for him to use in playing "tack yin." Or maybe it would be candy!

Ti clasped his little yellow hands ecstatically across his "shom," as the Chinese call the blouse.

But it does not do to clasp one's hands too suddenly when one is sitting on the end of a board in the air! Ti lost his balance, screamed, caught at the board, and fell over, down into the mud below! Oh, it was dreadful! His thick-soled shoes and blue trousers disappeared in the mud! The ends of his "shom" spread out over the mud, and he screamed a scream that would have been

"Do not fall," called Uncle Lum Lee.

intelligible to American as well as Chinese ears. Uncle Lum Lee had long since disappeared, but See Yow heard — old See Yow, who was going through the encampment to one of the buildings that had a shrine, such as a joss-house has. He was intending to put some incense sticks before the shrine, for he knew the proverb of his people, "In passing over the day in the usual way there are four ounces of sin." Yet his idea of "sin" was very different from the Christian idea. When he heard the scream he did not wait to go to the shrine, but hurriedly called to others near. There was a loud chattering, and at last little Ti was scooped out of the mud, as if he were a new and valuable variety of clam. He

Chinese Fishing Hamlet.

TI: A STORY OF CHINATOWN.

left one thick-soled shoe buried far out of sight, and he was borne away by old See Yow to be cleaned up again.

While he scraped and comforted, the old man told Ti how convenient it would have been to-day, if he had been one of the feathered people, for then he could have flown, when he found himself dropping into the mud. See Yow really believed that there are feathered people somewhere in the world, for he had been taught so, when he was a boy long ago, by a man from Swatow in China.

"The feathered people are gentle, and they are covered with fluffy down, and have wings," said See Yow, "and they sing."

Ti listened and watched the scraping off of his shoe.

The old man kept on talking about the feathered people. "If one wishes to visit that nation, he must go far to the southeast and then inquire," he finished, in the words of the tale as he had learned them.

By this time Ti was quite as clean as he could be made in so short a time. See Yow was always a kind, lovable old man.

"When the junk comes in, I will give you a piece of the present my father brings me," said Ti gratefully.

Old See Yow smiled. "May the Five Blessings come upon you!" he answered affectionately. "Surely you were a child that neither learned to walk nor speak early nor had teeth early!"

Now as certain Chinese believe that a child who does these things early has a bad disposition and will grow up unlovable, what See Yow said was very complimentary. And as the Chinese "Five Blessings" are health, riches, long life,

Old See Yow.

love of virtue, and a natural death, the old man wished the best things he knew for Ti. But to himself he smiled at little Ti's promise about the present, and thought, "Some presents will not bear dividing! It is but a child's promise. I shall have nothing."

But little Ti meant what he promised.

He would certainly give a piece of his present to kind old See Yow.

The little boy stayed with the shrimp-curers till the slow waters of the bay climbed again over the mud-flats toward the fishing-hamlet. Then the men on the junk out in the bay hoisted sail, and slowly the junk came toward the shore. But about three hundred yards from the shore, it ran aground in the mud. Small boats began to ply between the junk and the shore, however, and on one of these boats came Ti's father. He had not left Ti's present on board the junk with the load of salt, either. The present was inside of the father's blouse.

How Ti gazed, as his father fumbled in his blouse and brought out his present! It was a pair of bright, pink, American stockings! Oh, they were so bright and pink and pretty! The boy was delighted. He had never had anything but common white stockings to show above his low, thick-soled shoes before. The new pink stockings were clocked with silk up their sides, and to little Ti they seemed very beautiful.

He smiled with happiness, for Chinese small people when "dressed up" like to wear pretty colors. Then suddenly he remembered something. Had he not said he would divide his present — whatever it should be — with old See Yow? The little lad's smile vanished. Must he give away half of his beautiful new pink pair of stockings? What good was half a pair of stockings?

But the boy's father was still fumbling in his blouse, and a moment later he brought out some Chinese candy. Putting this into Ti's hands, he brought out something else.

"I saw the teacher woman in the city," he told in Chinese, and she said, 'Here is something for little Ti! Tell him to fasten it up by a street door, so that all the fishing-people will see it!'"

But the father frowned a little, as he said this, though he handed Ti the teacher's gift, which was a piece of red paper on which were some Chinese words in black characters. Ti's father did not like the city teacher woman very well, yet he had brought the paper safely because he thought that the little boy might like its red color. The words on the red paper seemed strange to him. He did not know what they meant.

"I will give this red paper to See Yow," resolved Ti, taking the paper. "Then I shall not have to give him one of my pink stockings! He may have some of my candy, too."

He ran away to find See Yow. The kind old man admired the pink stockings, refused the candy, but took the red paper. He tried to read what was printed on it in Chinese characters, but he did not understand. He puzzled over it quite a while.

Ti stood by, watching. "What does it say?" he asked.

"They are new words," answered old See Yow.

He read them aloud slowly: "'Come unto me, all ye that labor and are heavy laden, and I will give you rest.'"

Ti did not know what they meant. The teacher woman in the great California city where he used to live several years ago had spoken to him once about Christ, but he was a very little fellow then, and now he did not remember much she had said. So he could not help See Yow to understand the words on the red paper.

"The teacher woman said to put the paper up by a door where everybody can see," stated Ti in Chinese.

So See Yow held the red paper and went along slowly to the hut where he and some other Chinamen lived. Above and beside the outside of the door were already pasted red or yellow papers with inscriptions that said various things in Chinese. One paper said: "May we never be without wisdom." Another paper read, "Good hope," and another, "Good will come to us," and another, "May heaven give happiness."

But none of them held any such words as the teacher woman's red paper that See Yow's wrinkled old hands pasted now among the other inscriptions.

Back and forth through the narrow, dirty little street that ran through the hamlet went the Chinese men and women and children. They were all so busy with the shrimp-curing and the fish-drying and the household work that they hardly looked at See Yow's red paper. Once in a while a man stopped to look, but he did not know what the words meant. Some of the Chinamen who had once lived down in the city had heard of the Americans' Christ, but had not paid much attention. Many of the Chinese had lived in different fishing-villages for years, and had never had any one to teach them of Christ. See Yow had lived in California many years. He had wandered around through Chinese mining-camps and fishing-villages, but in the mining-camps there was no teaching of Chinese about Christ, and after all these years in a Christian land, the poor old man was in as dense ignorance of Christianity as when he came from his native land. This whole fishing-camp where he now lived knew little more of Christ than if it had been in China.

After seeing the paper pasted up by the door, Ti had run off with his own precious pink stockings. But old See Yow stood still and looked awhile at the red paper, and tried to think what the words meant. At last he shook his head slowly, saying as he turned away:

"They are new words. They are new words!"

Yet there those words of eighteen centuries stood on See Yow's shabby old outward wall, and hither and thither went the ignorant, hard-working Chinese people, who did not know the meaning of them.

CHAPTER II.

THE CALL FOR "CHOCK CHEE."

THERE was great excitement in the fishing-hamlet. There were six white men — yes, six — who had come to the hamlet, and no one knew wherefore!

Outwardly the Chinese were busy about their usual work, but inwardly they thought of little except the six white visitors and their errand. White men seldom came here, for there was no direct communication between the isolated hamlet and the city save by the Chinese junk's irregular trips. But the six white men had come in another vessel, now waiting in the bay. Some thought they had come to collect poll tax.

"I have paid poll tax many times," said Kim Tong in Chinese.

"Perhaps they have come to hunt for some bad Chinaman, to put him in jail," suggested Lin Tan.

The six white men walked around, apparently noting how many Chinamen there were in the camp, and what their occupations were. They looked at those who were splitting wood, and those who were mending nets, and those who were doing cooking, and those who were grinding shrimp shells and mixing them with sawdust. Great quantities of these ground shells and sawdust were sent to China, there to be used as a fertilizer of land. The six strangers looked at some

"I HAVE PAID POLL TAX MANY TIMES," SAID KIM TONG.

of the large nets. About a hundred such nets belonged to the fishing hamlet. Two or three Chinamen were making mattresses of red and white cloth, and the white men looked at these workers.

None of the dwellers in the little hamlet seemed outwardly to object to the white men's seeing all they wished to see. The Chinese were peaceful, but they did have a desire to know what was coming. They knew this unexpected visit meant something.

The white men peered into various little buildings, and saw in two or three of them such shrines as the Chinese erect for joss-worship.

"Religion isn't entirely neglected here!" said one of the visitors to another, laughingly.

"You'll find joss-shrines anywhere where you find Chinese living, I guess," answered the other.

They had gone around near the wharf again.

"It's an opportune time for us to come on our business," said a third white man, looking at the Chinese junk next the wharf. "Even their junk isn't out in the bay."

"It wouldn't be so much matter, if it were out there," said another. "These Chinese have a regular system of signals. They run up red and green and white flags on the flag-pole over that house yonder, and they could signal a junk to come in from the bay back to this place, if necessary. So it wouldn't hinder us from getting the Chinamen all together, unless the junk was too far out to see the signals. But probably all are here who

"Why have these men come?" said one Chinaman.

live here, now. We'd better begin pretty soon."

The men then went a little farther and gazed at the Chinamen who were attending to fish. Before the very faces of the white men the Chinese kept on talking together about why these visitors had come. They felt safe in talking their own language. They did not know that some of these men understood Chinese and knew what was being said about them.

"Why have these men come?" said one Chinaman. "Perhaps they will survey the shore for some purpose. Do they think they can take away our fishing-village?"

Finally, when the visitors had walked around the camp and had satisfied themselves that all the men usually employed were there, one of them went to the Chinese "boss" of the fishing-hamlet and told him to call all the men together.

"Chock chee," demanded the white man; and immediately the camp was astir, for "chock chee" meant the certificate a Chinaman must have to show that he had been legally admitted to this country.

Little Ti stood and looked at the commotion that ensued. Some of the Chinese hurried to their bunks and brought back their certificates. Others were very cross at having to stop their work, and would not go and get "chock chee" till command after command had been given.

"You all come here," said one white man in Chinese; and the Chinamen gathered in a group.

Then the six men began carefully to examine the certificates and compare the photograph on each with the Chinaman who presented it. As fast as the men and the certificates were looked at, the Chinese were told to stand aside, so that by and by there were two groups of Chinamen. The white men were carefully looking for fraudulent certificates.

Ti watched, for he was somewhat alarmed by something he heard one of the Chinamen say — that the men had brought a genuine "chock chee" with them, so as to have a standard by which they might detect any forged certificates; and though the white men had not come to find a real criminal, but only to discover anybody who had violated the law of "chock chee," yet they were so careful in comparing the genuine certificate with those shown by the Chinamen, that there was an impression made among the suspicious, waiting Chinese that perhaps, after all, there had been a murder committed by a Chinaman somewhere in the State, and these men were looking for the murderer.

Ti heard the Chinese about him murmuring various conjectures as to whom had been killed and where it had occurred. There were so many surmises that he felt frightened. He knew his father would have to come before those six men very soon, and he did not know what the men might do to him.

The little fellow grew so scared that he wanted to run away and hide himself in the building that was used as a sail loft and a place for storing the ropes and tackle belonging to the junk and other boats. But he stayed, because he watched for his father's turn to come before the white men. He knew that some of the Chinamen were out of temper. One of them had even kicked over a little dwarf pine that sat in a dish by his hut. But there was no use in being cross when the call was for " chock chee."

Ti knew from his father's looks that something was the matter. Uncle Lum Lee was safe. He had his certificate.

When it came his father's turn to go before the six white men, Ti tried to see between two old Chinamen. He thrust his little queued head under the Chinaman's arm and looked. Before the white men stood his father, talking briskly in English of his own.

"Me leave 'chock chee' in city," he said. "Him velly good number one 'chock chee!' No have him here. Leave him with my cousin in city."

"Very well," answered one of the men. "Then I arrest you. I will take you down to the city, and you may find 'chock chee' there and show me. Stand here."

Ti's father did not object at all. He had known, as soon as he heard the white men's errand, that he would have to go back to the city with them. Such a visit as this was very unexpected, and Ti's father told himself that he would always keep his "chock chee" within reaching distance hereafter.

Three other men were in the same predicament. Little Ti hardly understood. He knew that Uncle Lum Lee looked disgusted with his father.

When the examination was over, Ti's father, and the three other men whose certificates were missing, went and changed their clothes from fishing garments to others more appropriate for a visit to the city. The other Chinamen went back to their work, but these four

A Dwarf Pine.

came to the men on the net-drying platform.

"You all sure you got 'chock chee' in city?" asked one of the men.

"Yes," answered the four Chinamen.

They had thought the city a safer place to keep their certificates than here in the fishing-hamlet. They looked to see what their captors were going to do. The men began talking among themselves, and the Chinamen waited. During the long time that it had taken to carefully examine each one's "chock chee," the tide had gone out, and the white men would be forced to wait for its return, before they could start for the city.

"Tide's out. Got to wait," explained one of the men to the Chinese.

"Will they kill him?" Ti asked.

The four captives acquiesced, and sat down with their captors on the net-drying platform. The sun shone warm upon them, and the men stared at the great nets, and said something once in awhile to one another. None of them knew that a pair of frightened childish eyes was watching from shore.

The other more fortunate Chinamen of the hamlet did not seem to be much concerned about the fate of the four who had not been able to satisfy the white men about "chock chee." But Ti, who understood very little about the reason for any certificate, could not bear to go away out of sight of the net-drying platform where his father was — who knew what those white men were going to do to him?

The little boy's heart beat heavily with fear. He went behind a small hut on the edge of the fishing-hamlet, and peered out, keeping watch of his father and the three other prisoners.

"I don't know what they do to my father!" worried Ti, winking back the tears from his black eyes.

The men on the platform all seemed to be waiting for something. Ti did not know what it was, for he had not looked at the water of the bay. He kept his eyes fixed on his father. He expected to see something dreadful happen, but nothing occurred. At last the boy came out from his hiding place and set about finding out what was to be.

"What will they do to my father?" he asked one of the Chinamen.

"Take him to the city."

"Will they kill him?" he questioned, with a child's unreasoning fear.

The Chinaman shook his head.

"He come back," he said.

And Ti was comforted. "Me go, too," he thought, with new inspiration.

It had been a long time, about two years, since he had been to the city to see his cousin, a boy younger than himself. His father had been promising to take him sometime.

Ti now ran to the net-drying platform, and asked his father's permission. His father spoke to the white men.

"Oh, yes," said one. "Take the little fellow, if you want to! But don't take him unless you're sure you've got 'chock chee' in city. If you haven't 'chock chee' there, you're going to be in big trouble, and you don't want any boy along!"

"Me got number one 'chock chee' in city," reiterated Ti's father.

"All right," said the white man; and Ti ran to his uncle's wife to be dressed for the journey. His mother was dead, so Uncle Lum Lee's wife dressed him.

He was a gorgeous little Chinaman by the time his best clothes were on. His ordinary calico apron that he wore over his every-day "shom" was discarded, and his little body was stuffed out with many blouses, worn one over another in Chinese fashion. His outside blouse was bright yellow, and his trousers were green. They were tied about his ankles, but this did not hide the fact that he wore the things that he was most proud of, his new pink American stockings!

The little lad was ready long before there was any need of it, and he stood on the net-drying platform, a bright little figure in yellow and green and pink. The white men, the four Chinamen, and Ti, sat on the platform and waited for the tide. After a while one of the men yawned and rubbed his eyes.

"This 'chock chee' business is slow," he said.

An old figure in a shabby blue shom and trousers came down to the net-drying platform.

"Here comes a real old Celestial," said one white man.

Old See Yow came slowly on. He stopped.

"Kunghi, kunghi!" said old See Yow; meaning, "I respectfully wish you joy."

"Kunghi, kunghi, old man," said one of the men good-naturedly. "What can I do for you? Have you come to beguile our weary hours?"

"You talk Chinese," said old See Yow respectfully in his own tongue. "Can you also read it?"

"Some," answered the man.

"Will you come?" asked See Yow, beckoning. "I wish to show you something."

The man rose lazily and smiled. The time was long, and there were enough others to attend to the four Chinese. So he followed See Yow along the platform, off to the shore, through the narrow street, till they came to the old man's door. There, pasted up beside the entrance, was the new red paper that Ti had given him.

The old Chinaman pointed to the paper.

"Can you read it?" he asked in Chinese.

The man looked at the red placard. He studied it a little and then he nodded.

"You no read it?" he asked.

See Yow nodded. "I read," he said, "but the center of my heart does not understand. What is it the words say?"

The man read it: "Come unto me, all ye that labor and are heavy laden, and I will give you rest."

"You no sabe that?" he asked.

See Yow shook his head. No, he did not understand.

Somewhere in the depths of the visitor's memory something stirred. He remembered a boyhood when his mother read such verses. He remembered when he, too, read them. Little had he read such words in the years of manhood, but he knew what that red paper meant. Yes, he knew. He hesitated. He was glad his companions were not present to listen to his explanation.

"Jesus Christ said that," he explained in Chinese. "You know Jesus Christ?"

See Yow shook his head. He did not know anything about Jesus Christ.

The man stood and looked at the paper.

"Where did you get it?" he asked.

See Yow explained.

The other laughed a little.

"Very good paper," he said, and turned away.

Old See Yow looked puzzled and disappointed.

"What is it the words say?" he asked anxiously in Chinese. "What is it they say?"

But the man was walking down the narrow street. He did not care to talk about the words any more.

See Yow stood and looked at the red paper in a distressed way. Something in his heart cried out for the meaning of those words, but there was nobody to tell him what they meant.

"They are new words," he repeated despairingly. "They are new words."

There was a puzzled wistfulness in the old eyes. The strange man had said that it was a "very good paper." See Yow gazed at the paper respectfully. He would keep it there. Perhaps it was a charm to ward off evil spirits, as pieces of embroidered silk may keep evil spirits away, if the silk is hung near a bed.

Meantime the stranger had gone back to the net-drying platform. The men he had left there were talking together. One of them looked up.

"What did your old Chinaman take you off to see?" he asked laughingly.

"Just a paper," answered the other, as he walked down to the end of the platform, and stood alone a few minutes, looking out at the slow-coming tide.

"I didn't come down here to preach a sermon!" he told himself uneasily, trying to forget how old See Yow's face had looked. "'Chock chee' is more in my line. I wish that tide would hurry!"

He looked off at the distant horizon. Perhaps he saw something there besides low-lying haze. Perhaps he saw a little boy beside his mother's knee. Perhaps, too, he heard something besides the indistinct sound of conversation behind him and the cry of sea-gulls. Perhaps he heard that mother's voice reading out of an old Book. Presently he turned and went back to the others. By and by the tide came up, and the men and the four Chinese went off together with Ti. After a while the little Chinese fishing-hamlet faded, and Ti could see it no more.

It was wonderful to the little boy to be really going to the city! He stood on the boat and looked out at the sparkling, ruffled water. On and on they went, and he saw a sea-gull, and the wind blew brisk and salt, and he laughed at the spray that flew in his face. And then, after they had been sailing quite a time, he lifted his eyes and saw in the distance the smoke of an American steamboat. He was delighted. It was only a foretaste of the wonderful things he was going to see, he knew. He was going to the city!

But little Ti did not know what things should befall him there, and that he would not see the Chinese fishing-hamlet again for two whole years. Perhaps, if he had known, he would have turned and looked once more in the direction in which the fishing-hamlet lay.

But he did not think of such a thing as his staying away more than a few days. He stood looking at the smoke of the American steamboat, and the wind blew his pink-plaited little queue over his shoulder, and the spray lit on his bright yellow "shom" and green trousers, and his almond eyes took in everything.

"You're a regular little sailor," said one of the men in English.

But Ti did not understand. He knew only a very little English, for he had not had anybody to talk that language with at the fishing-hamlet, and he had forgotten many words he once had known when he lived in the city as a very little boy. Besides, he did not want to talk now. He was going to the great city, and he was so happy!

But, alas! back in the Chinese fishing-hamlet, old See Yow went to and fro, as ignorant and unsatisfied as ever. The "center of his heart" was yet wistfully longing for something, he knew not what. The "very good paper" with its message was not understood. Alas, that "chock chee" had been more in the white man's line!

CHAPTER III.

KWONG GOON.

THE city reached, Ti's father found his certificate and made his peace with the "chock chee" men. Then the two went to Ti's uncle's, and the boy was happy with his

16   TI: A STORY OF CHINATOWN.

little cousins in the small rooms above and back of the uncle's store, that was hung with gay Chinese lanterns, and had shelves and cases filled with Chinese dolls, and rice paper pictures, and little storks and frogs, and beautifully made boxes, and white silk handkerchiefs such as Americans buy.

It was a great change for Ti, coming from his little fishing-hamlet to this great city. His aunt, Ah Cheng, was glad to see him, and she began to cook some meat in Chinese cooking oil for the visitors. She turned the meat with a couple of red chopsticks while it was cooking, and into a kettle that contained some more cooking oil she threw the wet leaves of some vegetable. The leaves, beginning to cook, made a great spluttering in the hot oil on top of the charcoal range, and Ti thought how good dinner would be.

His aunt, Ah Cheng, was very pleasant, and told him he ought to have come to the city before, to visit his little cousin, baby Hop, who was now two years old, but whom Ti had never before seen. And then Aunt Ah Cheng told him how nice a birthday feast they had had for baby Hop when he was four weeks old. Chinese babies have a feast when they are four weeks of age. The other cousin, Hop's brother Whan, was five years old.

Ti went to the little front balcony and

looked out. Across the street he could see a Chinaman standing behind a small table set on the sidewalk. The table had a red, black-stained cover, and the man was a fortune-teller.

On a farther building were two enormous red and green lanterns. All of the people who lived along here were Chinese. Over at the corner was a Chinese butcher's shop, where pork and vegetables were for sale. One shallow, round basket on the sidewalk contained a quantity of white, dry watermelon seeds, such as the Chinese eat. Another basket held beans that had been made to sprout and put forth runners about two inches long. The runners and beans were alike very pale and were tender for eating.

Ti turned around and looked at the room in which he was standing. The outer room, in which his aunt was cooking, was one used in common for that purpose by other Chinese families living in this house, but the little room Ti stood in was exclusively that of Aunt Cheng's family. The little boy gazed at its furnishings. There was a shelf for the household gods, and there was a table with candles and incense-sticks. There were several stools, and a picture of the Chinese goddess of mercy, Kun Yam, the goddess that is so much worshiped by all Chinese women and girls, whether in China or America.

There was a bed made of boards, covered with a square of matting. Around the bed were some curtains, fastened with loops of Chinese money, "cash," and beside the curtains hung pieces of embroidered silk of different colors. These silken pieces were charms against evil spirits. Poor as the room was, it seemed beautiful to Ti, who had come so recently from his fishing-village.

He went back to the room where his aunt was cooking. Other women of different families were here now, and there was one quarrelsome woman among them. He did not like it so well as when his aunt was there alone, but his little

Chinese Fortune-teller's Table.

cousin, Whan, was ready to run down into the store with him, so together the two somewhat unacquainted cousins went below and peeped out the store door at the old Chinese fortune-teller and his red covered table, farther down across the

18   TI: A STORY OF CHINATOWN.

street. It did not seem to be a very good day for the fortune-teller. He stood there without any customers.

"But it is not so every day," said little

CHINESE MUSICAL INSTRUMENTS.

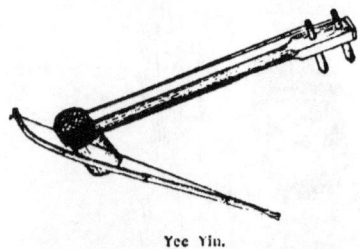

Yee Yin.

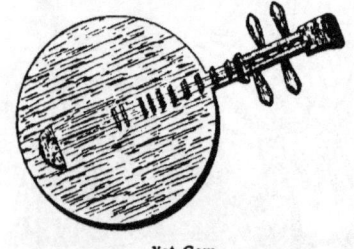

Yet Com.

Wong Sev.

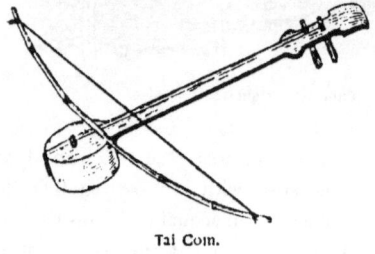

Tai Com.

Whan in Chinese to Ti. "He is very wise, and people go to him. Is there a fortune-teller at the fishing place where you live?"

"No," said Ti, who was greatly impressed by the wonders of the city.

The two children stepped out on the street. Here and there were other Chinese children, some with their parents, some alone on errands. There were many Chinamen going back and forth. Some, who had been to the butcher's, carried little cornucopias of brown paper containing small quantities of meat. Most such Chinese people had very little quantities of vegetables, too. There was a queer sound of music in the air. That is, the music would have been strange in American ears. Some one in the upper story of an opposite building was playing a stringed musical instrument.

Ti stood and looked over at the unfortunate fortune-teller. But he did not seem to be much depressed by his lack of customers, and there was so much else to see and hear that Ti forgot about him. The stringed instrument had been joined by other Chinese musical instruments, and the little boy stared up at the higher window opposite and listened. But his cousin Whan did not like this. He pulled Ti farther on the street.

"Come and see," said he, bent on showing his country cousin the sights.

But Ti would listen for a minute or two. He thought the music was very fine, though it was squeaky. But soon the squeaking instruments were aided by a much more powerful one, for some other

TI: A STORY OF CHINATOWN.

player joined in with a loud sound of metal beaten, as of a kettle-drum.

Ti saw an old Chinaman sitting on a box on the sidewalk. He had another little box before him, and he was an opium pipe mender. He was busy mending and cleaning part of such a pipe — jin-ten — now.

Around the corner sat a Chinese cobbler, working on the street. He held a blue, thick-soled Chinese shoe, and hummed a funny little song. There were some pieces of leather soaking in a small tub beside him, and on the side of the box before him there was a red paper with Chinese characters. The cobbler had a board put up at one side of his open-air shop, and he looked at Ti and little Whan in a friendly way.

Ti gazed into a Chinese barber shop, and saw the barber shaving a customer's head. The customer held up a little tin box, and every time the barber clipped off any hair, he dropped it into this tin. Another barber was cleaning out the interior of a customer's ear with a little black instrument.

Not far off was a Chinese druggist's

Chinese Cobbler.

shop. In the window were two bottles of "horned toads" in alcohol, and, peering into the store, Ti saw a Chinaman sitting, working the handle of a machine up and down. He seemed to be cutting roots to pieces, and the machine appeared to work somewhat as a machine for thinly slicing dried beef does in an American grocery store.

The two boys went on to a Chinese vegetable shop, where some yellow squares of bean curd were piled for sale. Each square of curd was marked with a Chinese character, and the curds were noticeable on account of their yellow color.

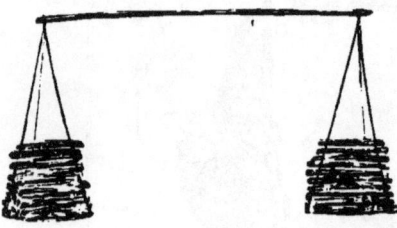

Chinese manner of carrying wood in San Francisco.

Long pieces of sugar cane, brought from China, stood up against the side of the building, like so many fishing poles or pieces of bamboo. There were cut pieces of sugar cane, too, about seven inches long, for sale, two pieces for five cents.

Ti gazed at a cage of turtles slowly crawling about their prison. There were some big crabs, too, in a receptacle, one lying on his back. The crabs made Ti feel more at home. He had seen so many of them at the fishing village.

Near by was a Chinese shop for dried fish. Here on a corner was an old scribe, writing a letter for a Chinese coolie. He wrote with a brush that he held upright and moved mostly by his little finger. Ti and Whan looked at this scribe's writing with great respect. In a few minutes the letter was written, the coolie paid the scribe and went away.

"We must go home," said little Whan in Chinese to Ti. "My mother will have cooked the dinner."

They turned around and went back toward Whan's father's store. The two children looked again at the vegetable shop as they went by it, and Whan said that once the Chinese vegetable seller had given him a piece of sugar cane to eat. Both boys would have liked some sugar cane. They looked at the vegetable man's little boy, and lingered near his shop a minute, but the vegetable seller was too busy to notice.

Ti turned away. He peeped into another street, and beheld a sight that horrified him — a house with five great gilded teeth swinging in the balcony before the house! He gazed with horror at those big teeth. He had never before known about Chinese dentists, and those swinging, monstrous teeth filled him with fearful conjectures of what was done in that house. He turned and ran.

Little Whan could not imagine what had frightened his cousin so. He ran after, calling. Ti ran in the wrong direction, not toward his uncle's store, and nearly plunged down the stairs into a cellar below the sidewalk, where wood was for sale by Chinamen. Looking down the stairs, the passers could see the wood tied in little bundles for purchasers.

TI: A STORY OF CHINATOWN. 21

There was a bright new axe visible in the cellar. A Chinaman came along the street, carrying an amount of wood at each end of a pole hung across his shoulder, as a Chinese vegetable peddler carries his baskets, except that the two piles of wood were not in baskets, but were kept in place at each end of the pole by a Chinese contrivance.

Whan caught up with Ti, and, grasping his shoulder, said, "You go the wrong way. Why did you run?"

But Ti would not tell, for he was already a little ashamed to have been frightened over the big swinging teeth. He felt as if he were an ignorant little country Chinaman. No doubt small Whan, five years old, had often seen that house with the teeth, and was not scared; and here was he, Ti, a boy eight years old, afraid of something that did not terrify his little cousin! So Whan did not get any answer to his question.

But it was time for dinner, and Ti was quite ready to run home. The boys had dinner together, without any sugar cane, but Ti did not care. The Chinese greens and the meat tasted very good, and he ate rice, too.

Ti's father thought that he and his

Chinese Dried-fish Shop.

little boy would stay a few days and visit. It was the time of the feast of Kwong Goon, that heathen deity who, the Chinese believe, has much to do with the dead. Ti's father had thought of its being the time of the feast, and he had been all the more willing to come down to the city with the "chock chee" men.

The next day after arriving in the city, Ti and his father, and little cousin Whan and the uncle, went to a joss-house to see and to carry gifts for the festival. Those Chinese who had relatives that had died since the last Kwong Goon festival, brought prayer papers and joss sticks to the altar. Candy, tea, cigars and dried fish were laid before Kwong Goon. Well might the Chinese fear him, according to their religious belief, for he is the deity who is supposed to devour the bodies of irreligious Chinamen.

Much money had been spent on this festival. Little Ti, looking at the altar of Kwong Goon, saw it resplendent with candles and gilt censers. The gilded altar pieces were imported ones, and in this joss-house in the Chinese part of an American city, the Chinese high priest intoned the services for the souls of dead Chinamen.

Ti and his folks were near the shrine. If this had not been so, perhaps something would not have happened. As it was, five-year-old Whan came to great grief. Notwithstanding the holiness of the altar, the Chinese men occasionally took cigars from a tray that lay before the shrine. Seeing this, little Whan reached out his tiny yellow hand and helped himself to a piece of dried fish that had been offered to Kwong Goon.

Woe to little Whan! What a crime was this! The Chinese women who were about him pounced down on the little boy and nearly choked him, trying to get that piece of fish, for he had put it into his mouth, and the women were determined to get the fish before he could swallow it. They forced his mouth open. One woman had her bony fingers tightly around his throat. Another had seized the end of the piece of fish. Whan struggled and gasped. Ti looked on in alarm, lest his little cousin should be choked. But the women got the fish.

The tumult subsided. Great Kwong Goon was honored by an offering of punk sticks, and little Whan, the beginner of this confusion, offended against the proprieties of the occasion no more. Perhaps what he had done would have been forgotten, had not something happened to him within the next few days, something that his parents regarded as the result of Whan's act at the Kwong Goon festival.

What happened was this. The festival continued through the week, and Ti and his father stayed, for the father had some matters he wanted to attend to in the city. Now, about five days after his visit to the shrine of Kwong Goon, little Whan was taken ill. He was languid and slightly feverish. He could not swallow his rice without pain and difficulty.

TI: A STORY OF CHINATOWN. 23

"It is because you tried to eat a piece of the fish belonging to Kwong Goon," said his mother. "This is your punishment."

Little Whan, who felt very miserable, supposed that what his superstitious mother said was true. He did not know that he had been exposed to diphtheria, and that he would probably have had the disease anyway, if he had not gone to the festival. He resolved that he would never offend Kwong Goon again.

Whan felt no better after his resolve, however, and his father thought that the disease must be produced by some angry spirit. So that night the father went outside the store with some pieces of Chinese money and a bowl of rice, and after prostrating himself several times before the invisible evil spirit, he threw the money and the rice at the place where he supposed the evil spirit to be. Then he went back into the house.

"You will be well now," he told Whan. "Lu-tsu, the medicine god, who pities the sick, will help you."

But Whan was not well. Seeing this, his father made up his mind to go to a Chinese drug store, although he would not

The Vegetable Man's Little Boy.

stay there for any other business than that pertaining to the place, for fear that the evil spirits that produce sickness might be lurking among the medicines. So, having seen the sign in Chinese, "Bad Spirits Not Admitted," he got Whan some medicine from the "Hall of Joyful Relief," as the Chinese characters on the apothecary's shop denoted it to be. But the "Hall of Joyful Relief" did not help the little boy, so his father got some medicine from the "Promise Life Palace," and the "Hall for Multiplying Years," and the "Great Life Hall," and from a place where the board read in Chinese. "Wo Ki Ying feels the pulse and writes prescriptions for internal and external disease." Moreover the father consulted one of the Chinese fortune-tellers, who looked at the sick child's nose and said it was like a dog's, and for that reason Whan would live long. According to this fortune-teller's rule, "A man with a dog's nose will live long."

Moreover, the friendly Chinese butcher, who had recently come from China, gave Ti's father a cow's tooth which had been found in a field near Swatow, and which, the butcher said, if brought into a dwelling and put on the shelf of the gods, would keep demons from entering.

With all this, little Whan did not seem to get better.

CHAPTER IV.

LITTLE WHAN.

DURING Whan's sickness the other children were not kept away from him. It was not the Chinese custom to do that.

When the teacher — who was not the person who had sent the paper to the fishing camp, but another teacher — came through the district and saw little Whan, she knew that something serious was the matter. She said to his father, "Your boy is sick. You should get an American doctor."

"It is Kwong Goon who makes Whan sick," said Ah Cheng, the child's mother. "Kwong Goon will punish him for taking the fish! His throat is sick."

But the father did as the teacher said. He sent for an American doctor.

"Your boy has diphtheria," said the doctor, as he looked at little Whan. "That's what ails him."

The doctor told the father to keep the sick boy in a room separate from the other children.

"Yes," said the father stupidly, and he looked at the doctor and wondered if, after all, it would not have been much better to have gone again to the "Hall of Joyful Relief" and got some more Chinese medicine, than to have called this American doctor. For what was the reason why Whan should be shut up in a room by himself? Would not the evil spirits that make sickness come to him? What a singular thing!

The father looked suspiciously at the doctor and his medicine. It was Kwong Goon who had made Whan ill, no doubt, and was it likely that putting the boy off in a room by himself would cure him? What did this American doctor know about Kwong Goon, anyhow?

The doctor saw the father's distrustful look, and tried to explain as best he could in English.

"Do you not see?" asked he. "If your boy has diphtheria, your baby might take it, and so might the cousin from the country. You must keep Whan in a room by himself."

"Yes," said the father. "Yes."

"Be sure to do it," reiterated the doctor.

"Yes," said the father; and, after the doctor had gone, he told his wife, who had not seen the doctor, for he had not been allowed to come to the living-room upstairs, but only to enter the store.

But the next day, when the teacher came back, she found that Whan's mother had not done as the doctor said. She meant to do the best for her children, poor Ah Cheng! but she did not understand about infection.

"You must put Whan in a different room, away from the other children," said the teacher kindly, and she showed the mother how.

Whan stayed separate till after the teacher went away. Then, somehow, in the midst of the work, the three children all were together again. There was nothing before the doorways of the rooms,

Chinese Festival of Kwong Goon.

anyhow, except thin red curtains. Ti and Hop wanted to be with Whan constantly, and the mother thought that keeping the sick child separate was only an American notion, anyway, and not of much importance. It seemed too bad to separate the children, when they liked one another so well. In pure kindness, Ah Cheng allowed the three to be together.

Toward evening the teacher came again. She was alarmed over Whan, and stayed to watch by him, but the ignorant mother slept. In the morning the father and mother were frightened about the sick child, for they saw how very much worse he was. They lighted tapers and burned incense, hoping to make him better, and to appease the evil spirit that they felt sure was tormenting him. Diphtheria is common enough in China, sometimes.

But Whan grew worse. He could not drink without strangling. He did not wish to eat.

By this time, two-year-old Hop and his cousin Ti were both taken with the same disease, diphtheria.

"It is Kwong Goon who does this," still said Whan's mother. "It is the god Kwong Goon."

But little five-year-old Whan was dying, though his mother did not realize it.

The teacher, who had been obliged to go herself for the American doctor and had not found him in, hurried now from the street into the narrow alley. Around it stood Chinamen as usual, talking. A Chinese woman with ankle ornaments like bracelets went into a doorway. The teacher nodded to the woman and hurried on. All these Chinese were used to seeing the teacher now, and they did not watch her suspiciously, as they had once done. They knew, now, that she was friendly, and she could talk their tongue.

The teacher hastened up the long outside narrow stairs that led to the rooms where Ti's aunt lived. A door at the top of the stairway had some Chinese characters on it. She rapped, said something in Chinese, and entered without waiting.

Directly in front of her, in the tiny, box-like entry, was what would look to American eyes like a large, rectangular tin for ashes. There were ashes in the tin, but there was a red paper on the wall above, and this was a place for worship of the gods.

The teacher did not stop an instant. She hurried through the narrow passage at the left. The passage was cut with several doors, hung with thin red curtains. A person could readily enter any room, but the teacher hastened to the one where Ti and Whan and Hop were. She had not meant to be away so long.

But she knew, now, before she entered the room, that One had been there before her. He who loves the children had looked not only upon little Whan in his pain and suffering, but on baby Hop, and was taking them to himself. The teacher heard wailing before she lifted the thin red curtain of the room. Little Whan was dead. The dreadful diphtheria had done its work, and when the teacher took baby Hop into her arms, she believed that the child would follow his brother soon.

The teacher did all she could. The American doctor came at last, but it was too late. In those last dreadful moments

Whan's Mother.

of baby Hop's life, his mother, poor Ah Cheng, prostrated herself before the old picture of the goddess of mercy, and prayed and sobbed.

"Oh, save my baby! Save my baby!" she sobbed wildly in Chinese. "Oh, Kun Yam, goddess of mercy, save my baby!"

The teacher's tears ran down her cheeks, as she saw the heart agony with which poor Ah Cheng sobbed and wrung her hands and prayed before that picture. But the dear little two-years-old baby in the teacher's arms drew a last, faint gasp, and the teacher saw with reverent awe the seal of death set itself on the baby face.

She laid down the little body and put the chubby brown hands gently together, and then went softly across the room, and knelt beside the poor wailing mother.

Ah Cheng lifted up her drawn, agonized face, and looked toward her child. As she realized what had happened, a cry of despair broke from her

Whan.

lips. She flung herself wildly down, and beat her head against the floor.

"Kun Yam! Kun Yam!" she wailed. "I shall never see them again! Both my sons are dead, and I shall never see them again! Kun Yam! Kun Yam!"

"Poor Ah Cheng! I am so sorry for you," said the teacher, slipping her arm around Ah Cheng and drawing her head down until it rested upon her shoulder. "I am so sorry for you, and there is One who is more sorry for you than anybody else can be, for He is here and knows our sorrow. It is Jesus, Ah Cheng, Jesus, who loves the children. Your children are with him and he will keep them safe. And, Ah Cheng, he loves you, too, and wants to comfort you."

Ah Cheng's sobbing grew a little quieter.

"You cry out to Kun Yam, Ah Cheng, because your heart must have help in this trouble; and Jesus is listening to every cry, and he can help you. He has taken the little ones to himself. Some day he will restore them to you, if you trust him and open your heart to his love, believing in him as your best Friend."

Then very lovingly and patiently did the teacher try to explain to the stricken mother that this Jesus is the one true God, and that he is close to us, though our eyes cannot see him.

The night that baby Hop died, Ti was too ill to know it. He did not comprehend the wailing. It had been a confused outburst of sound without any meaning to him, as he half dozed on his bunk. As feverish Ti lay there the next day, however, he looked continually at the teacher. Sometimes he seemed to himself to know her. Other times he thought he did not. There was an odor of much burning incense in the air. He felt very strangely. He wished he were back in the fishing village with his father and old See Yow and Uncle Lum Lee and the others. He had never felt so queer there. He did not know that he was sick. He only knew that sometimes the teacher sitting as he supposed by baby Hop seemed to turn into old See Yow, and sometimes she looked like his father. And sometimes the tapers that were lit seemed to whirl and change, as he had seen the moonlight on the waves near by the fishing village at night.

His throat hurt. He had not eaten his rice. His throat felt as little Whan said his felt that day at the feast of Kwong Goon, when the bony-fingered woman clasped his neck so tightly, to keep him from swallowing the piece of fish.

As Ti lay looking with feverish eyes, suddenly the teacher's face seemed to him to be that of the heathen deity, Kwong Goon. The child shuddered. He could not reason any more. He thought Kwong Goon's fingers were clasping the neck of this little sick Chinese boy, Ti himself.

"I did not touch your fish! Whan did it!" Ti struggled to cry out, but the words stopped in his throat.

Surely the great, the dreadful Kwong Goon would not make such a mistake!

TI: A STORY OF CHINATOWN.   29

He must know the difference between Ti and Whan!

He tried to shut his feverish eyes, but they would come open again, and every time he opened them he became more and more sure that it was not the teacher woman who sat there, but it must be Kwong Goon. Poor little Ti! He was becoming more and more feverish and confused. He did not have his right mind, or he would not have thought so foolish a thing, but the continual talk of his relatives about Kwong Goon, the last few weeks, had frightened him, and now his feverish brain was alarmed at seeing what he thought was Kwong Goon's face. The teacher did not know that the little boy lay there in a state of terror, or she would have sprung up and come to him. He opened his lips and tried to cry, "Go away, Kwong Goon! Go away!" He tried to say, "You must not kill me!" but something in his throat seemed to stop the words.

The imagined face seemed to come nearer. It was dreadful Kwong Goon. Ti tried to cry out, to escape. Kwong Goon came nearer.

"Go away!" the sick boy tried to scream. "Go away!"

But he could not speak. He felt as if he were choking. Suddenly he felt the teacher woman bending over him.

"Ti," she said gently in Chinese, "little Ti, what is it? Do not be afraid. Remember Jesus is here — Jesus that I told you about, Ti — Jesus who loves you. He is strong. He can keep you safe."

Ti could not answer. The teacher lifted him. He heard a wailing. There came a strong odor of incense. He gasped.

Then he did not remember things any

"A man with a dog's nose will live long," said the fortune-teller.

more for a while. Occasionally the teacher's face would show in the mist that seemed to surround him. One time it occurred to him to wonder why the teacher woman did not leave him any more and go to Hop. He tried to turn his head and look toward baby Hop. It took a good deal of trying, but at last he did turn his head. The place where the baby had lain was empty. Ti shut his eyes, and everything drifted away into mist again. At the fishing-hamlet he had sometimes seen the fog roll up the bay and cover everything from sight. So now everything vanished.

He did not know when the wailing-women came, and candles were burned, and afterwards Chinese imitation paper money was thrown away on the street, as the bodies of little Whan and little Hop were taken away to the Chinese burying ground far out toward the ocean.

In the days that came the Christian teacher woman stayed with Ti and did her best to comfort Ah Cheng. Whenever she could, she tried to teach her more about Jesus. But Ah Cheng was afraid to believe, for all her life she had feared the gods, and what the teacher told her seemed too good to be true.

Gradually Ti grew better. He was out of danger. His father, who knew from the epidemics of diphtheria in China how that disease can take away children, felt much relieved that Ti was growing better. He believed that diphtheria is caused by an evil spirit, and now he went to the joss-house and posted on the wall a red paper of thanksgiving for Ti's recovery.

According to the Chinese custom of wailing, little Whan and baby Hop were wailed for by their mother at a set time of day every seventh day for seven successive weeks. But it was no formal mockery of wailing with poor Ah Cheng. Sometimes Chinese people wail at the set time and then suddenly break off wailing and go about their work as if nothing had happened except that they had performed a duty. But Ah Cheng's mourning came from her heart, and many a time, besides the set wailing periods, she wept for her little children, and often in her loneliness she sobbed, "I shall never see them again!"

When Ti was well enough to be around again, his uncle and aunt besought his father, saying, "Let Ti stay with us a while! Whan is dead and Hop is dead. Let Ti stay to comfort us a while."

So Ti's father, pitying the lonely parents, went back to the fishing-hamlet alone, and Ti was left to live on with his uncle and aunt.

CHAPTER V.

A NEW ACQUAINTANCE.

THEY were very kind to Ti in his uncle's home. The Chinese are fond of children, and Ti had no mother at the fishing-hamlet to worry about him.

When the twenty-first day after the death of little Whan and Hop was passing, Ti's aunt looked very sorrowful. She spread a table with food, such as little Whan and Hop had liked in their lifetime. That night the doors were all left unlocked, and the uncle and Ti and his aunt went to bed. But Ah Cheng wept, for she believed that at midnight her little boys' spirits would return and she would not see them. But the doors must not be locked on her own children. They must be allowed to come in. The Chinese think that it is not till a person has been dead twenty-one days that he knows he is dead. Then he discovers it and is frightened. Crying out in alarm, he starts back to earth. Ti's aunt thought that her little boys would come back and take the essence of the food she had set out for them, and would go away again to the spirit world, leaving the substance of the food for the family to eat the next morning. No wonder that stricken Ah Cheng cried all night at the thought that her two little children came back, frightened, and she could neither see nor speak to them, and they went away again.

"I shall never see them again!" wept the poor mother through the night. "Kun Yam! Kun Yam! I shall never see them again!"

The teacher who had been so kind during the children's illness came often now to try to comfort their mother and teach her and Ti. But it seemed almost impossible for Ah Cheng to believe and so be comforted. She was very superstitious, and in this new home to which Ti had come, the "front door god," the "street god," the "floor god," the "kitchen god," the "bed god," the "roof god," the "water god," and the "sky goddess" were worshiped.

The teacher was very kind and pitiful to the poor mother.

"I want to tell you something, Ah Cheng," she said one day, when she had come in and found the heart-broken woman bowed before the old picture of the goddess of mercy, and Ti sitting soberly watching his aunt's tears and sobbing.

"I want to tell you something," she repeated. "A number of years ago there lived in China a girl who worshiped the goddess of mercy, as you worship her. After this girl had worshiped the goddess for twenty years, her mother lay dying. The mother told the family to make her ready and lay her away to die. So they dressed her in good clothes and, putting her on a board, laid her in another room to die. The mother died and was buried. The daughter felt very badly, but the goddess of mercy did not help in this great trouble."

Ah Cheng's wistful eyes were fixed on the teacher's face.

"No, the goddess did not help," repeated the teacher gently in Chinese. "The poor daughter had no hope of ever seeing her mother again. The only help she had was to go and lie on her mother's grave all day, in hope that she might dream of her at night. It was only in dreams that the poor daughter had any hope of ever seeing her dear mother's face again."

The tears filled poor Ah Cheng's eyes. She could not even go and lie on her children's graves, for they were away on the sand dunes out by the ocean, and she was a Chinese woman and must stay in the little rooms where she lived. How often she had longed to dream of her two little ones since they died!

"Let me tell you the rest of the story, Ah Cheng," said the teacher gently. "That poor daughter would not pray to the goddess of mercy any more, after her mother's death. Kun Yam had not helped in her time of great trouble, so now for seven years the daughter worshiped nothing. She kept the old picture of the goddess of mercy, but she did not worship it, and she was very unhappy.

"But one day she went to see a friend at a Christian hospital. At the hospital one of the helpers, noticing her sad face, began to talk to her about Jesus. She told her that Jesus could make her happy. She became very attentive, and when she went away the helper asked her to come again as soon as she could to hear more about Jesus.

"She came again and again, and as she learned about Jesus she learned to love him and great joy came into her heart.

"Jesus made the daughter happy, dear Ah Cheng, and it is Jesus who can help you. He wants you to learn to know him, so he can give you joy, too. He wants to make you happy even if you cannot now see your children. And then by and by when you die he wants to take you to a beautiful place where you will see him face to face, and your little ones, too, and where your children will never be taken from you again. But you need not be lonely and grieving till then. He wants to be with you right here in your home every day, to comfort and help you."

Ah Cheng cried, but she dared not believe. She was afraid of the gods. Oh, how she did wish she could see her little ones again and know this Jesus that the teacher told about! If only she could be sure they were safe and happy, as the teacher woman said! But Cheng's husband had said that the "Jesus doctrine" (religion) was not true. Poor Ah Cheng was sorely puzzled.

The teacher saw how it was. "Poor Ah Cheng!" she thought as she went away. "Poor, heart-broken creature! I will pray for her and help her to come to Jesus."

One day the teacher gave Ti a brown paper book, full of Chinese characters.

"Ti," she said, "your uncle loves you. Perhaps he will do for you what he will not do for me. Listen to me. This is a wonderful book. It is the Jesus book. and I give it to you. I want you to ask your uncle to read it. He will not read it for me, but you ask him. He loves you. He will do much for you."

So Ti, who loved the teacher because she had been good to him when he was sick, took the brown paper book and kept it carefully. It was not as pretty as the red paper the other teacher woman had sent to the fishing-hamlet, but he knew that this brown paper book must be something valuable, if this kind teacher said so.

But though Ti asked his uncle many

times, the uncle would not read the book, which was the New Testament in Chinese. But the little boy did not yet know the reason of that refusal.

He missed his two cousins very much. The teacher saw this, and she begged that the aunt and the uncle would let Ti go to a small daily Chinese Mission school with which she was connected. "He will be happy with the other children," urged the teacher, "and I will myself come for him every day and will bring him safely back after school."

But the uncle would not consent. "No," said he sternly. "Ti shall not go! The Jesus doctrine is very bad!"

He frowned at the teacher as he spoke. He knew what had happened in another Chinese family, he said, after a little boy had been allowed to go to the school. "The little boy's father," he said, "made the boy put the incense sticks up after the custom of Chinese worship. The boy was standing on a chair to put the incense sticks in place, but he did it very slowly. His heart was not in it, but he did it because he must obey his father. The boy's little brother said, 'He doesn't want to do it. He believes in Jesus.' And the father then struck the little boy who was putting up the incense sticks and pushed him off the chair. The boy cried a little, but it was true that he did not exactly wish to put up the incense sticks. Ti shall not become like that boy."

At this the teacher, fearing that she might be forbidden to come to the house if she said more, did not urge Ti's attendance on school. "But I do wish we could have him," she thought. "He is so bright, and already he understands a little of what I have tried to tell him about Christ. Still, I dare not talk about our school any more now! Poor little Ti!"

But she did not know that she would

Yun.

have Ti in school yet. In his loneliness it was not long till the little lad had become acquainted with a Chinese boy who lived near his uncle's store. The boy was several years older than Ti, and was named Yun. Yun went to an American public school, where he learned to read English. Late in the afternoons, he went to still another school, kept by a Chinaman, who taught boys how to read and write Chinese characters. Yun was a very different boy in one school from what he was in the other. In the morning and early afternoon public school, taught by Americans, he was a restless, fun-loving boy. In the late afternoon when he went to learn Chinese characters of the teacher brought from China, he dared not misbe-

Reading aloud the news.

have. Yun would have thought such a thing dreadful. Some of the Chinese boys who went to these schools wore certain "honorable" gowns, long and blue, and those who wore such a garment would not have disgraced it by misbehaving. Yun did not have one of these gowns, but in his ordinary Chinese dress he would not have behaved wrongly in the Chinese teachers' public school.

Ti, seeing Yun start off to attend schools so often, and knowing that he was learning Chinese characters, was greatly impressed, and believed that he knew a great deal. Yun's family believed in learning. His grandfather, who wore great goggles and occasionally smoked a pipe that was about a yard long, was reputed to be a very learned man; and Yun's father published a Chinese newspaper every week, in some rooms upstairs across the street from Ti's uncle's store. No wonder that the boy Yun must go to school so much and learn so many Chinese characters. He must become wise, like the others of his family.

Ti used to walk across the street, and stand at the Chinese printing-office stairway door, and listen to the Chinamen reading, for by the door were red and pink posters that told what the news was, and sometimes there were several men about the door, reading the news aloud. Ti could not read the Chinese characters, himself, of course, but he used to look at the bulletins and think he would read sometime.

When none of the men were around, the editor's boy, Yun, would sometimes proudly show off his knowledge to Ti by pointing out characters and telling their names, and Ti would listen and admire, and wonder at Yun's learning.

Innocent Ti did not notice that Yun was not wont to air his knowledge when men were by. Yun was crafty. He knew he could impress Ti, but he knew also that it would be a long time before he could become a good reader of Chinese, and it was wise to refrain from trying to show off before men who might laugh.

Occasionally Yun took Ti upstairs to the Chinese printing-office, and let him look in. He would see a man whose face showed marks which told that he had once had the "heavenly blossom," as some Chinese call smallpox. This pock-marked man Ti would see sitting engraving the stone from which the next week's paper was to be printed. The old-fashioned lithographic process was followed in getting out the paper. On the floor Ti would see scattered clippings from American or Chinese papers, and he would go away downstairs again, feeling how very ignorant he was, and how many, many things there were yet in this world for him to learn.

CHAPTER VI.

THE WORD "SHÜ."

THERE came a time when Ti was shocked out of his friendship for Yun. One afternoon, when Yun was going to the Chinese teachers' school, Ti was permitted to go, too, as a visitor. He had never been in a Chinese school, and he was very much impressed, as Yun knew he would be. There were two rooms of Chinese boys, studying under two Chinese teachers. Yun was in the room for less advanced scholars, but that made no difference with Ti's admiration for him. There were about twenty pupils in Yun's room. They were all boys, and they sat at desks and kept their hats on in the school-room. Some of the Chinese boys dressed in American clothes, but most wore their common, every-day dress.

The teacher, a dignified Chinaman on the platform in front of the school, wore a somewhat long, dark blouse and green trousers that were fastened about his ankles. His cap had a red button on top, and from a hook beside the teacher hung another blouse of his, lined with blue silk.

Ti sat at a desk, and listened, and looked. There was a great deal to listen to, for the Chinese boys studied out loud. It was rather startling when a boy who had been sitting listlessly at his desk would suddenly begin studying in a loud, shrill voice. But everybody was used to it. There was continually one boy after another carrying his brown paper book

of Chinese characters to the teacher's platform. The teacher would mark a certain place in the book with a red pencil, and the boy would begin to say the characters, and the teacher would go through with some sing-song recitation too, almost always, so that, taking the teacher, and the boy that was reciting, and the dozen or so other boys that were studying aloud, there was much noise in the room. Yet it was an orderly sort of noise, after all. None of the pupils misbehaved. Once a boy left his seat and spoke a short sentence to another boy, but this seemed to be no infringement of rules. The speaker went immediately back to his seat again.

"See me, what I do!" said Yun to Ti. With a proud heart Yun took his book and went to the platform. Giving the teacher the book, he turned his back to him, as was proper in reciting from memory, and began a somewhat long recitation in Chinese. Only once did the teacher have to correct him. Ti looked on in great admiration. When should he ever be able to "back the book" like that?

When Yun, proud of his success, came back to his seat, he proceeded further to impress Ti by preparing to write. Now Yun could not yet make Chinese characters without tracing them, but Ti watched his method of writing with great respect. On his desk he had what looked a good deal like a round box of hard shoe-blacking, such as bootblacks use. Yun's cake was not shoe-blacking at all, however, but dry ink, such as the other Chinese boys had. Toward one side of the round cake was a hole.

Yun left his desk, and, carrying the black cake of ink, went out the back door of the school-room. He returned with the hole in his ink-receptacle filled with water. Then he rubbed some of the water on his dry, round cake of ink. He took his book, which had leaves made of white paper that looked as thin as tissue paper, and yet, for all their thinness, not one leaf was torn. On the leaves were many red or black Chinese characters. At the left-hand end of the book were two of the transparent white leaves that had never been cut lengthwise. They were purposely left whole, though the top and bottom had been cut. In this way the two leaves made a kind of case.

Between these leaves Yun slipped a loose sheet of Chinese characters. Of course the characters showed through the almost transparent white paper. Then he took an implement that looked much like a sharpened wooden pencil that had small Chinese characters on pink paper pasted around the handle end of the implement. Yun rubbed the point of this writing implement on the wet cake of ink, and began to trace the Chinese characters showing through the thin white paper. He did this work with great accuracy.

Before going home, Ti obtained a peep into the other school-room where the older scholars were studying. The teacher of this room was not very pleasant-looking, he thought. He did not like that teacher so well as the one in Yun's room. This other teacher sat on a platform at the left-hand side of the room, instead of the front, and the scholars all had their hats on, and these boys studied out loud with more noise than the boys in the other room. On two desks were queer little green animals, made of some sort of ware, each looking somewhat like a horse with his head in the air. In the middle of the back of the "horse" was a round hole, for these animals were meant to contain water. If Yun had had such a "horse," he would not have had to carry his cake of ink out of the room to get water.

Back of all the scholars in this second room was a little table. Ti knew the purpose of it at once. Above the table was a picture-frame containing a red paper with large Chinese characters. Some sort of pink drapery was about the picture-frame, and two stiff bunches of what might be called artificial flowers were above. On the table below were tiny splints in a vase. The whole was a Chinese shrine, in honor of idol-worship. "To make it to joss," was Yun's explanation of the shrine.

As Ti, greatly impressed with his afternoon at the school, walked home with Yun, vainglorious Yun grew proudly boastful. Ti was so gentle and believing that he looked on these boastings as perfect truth. But at last Yun went too far in his talk. He said something that startled Ti.

"When I am a man, I shall know both English and Chinese," said he in Chinese proudly, "and I shall translate important news from the American newspapers for our honorable Chinese paper, as my father does now! Perhaps I shall be one of the men who look over the news of the steamers from China! I shall be very learned, and I shall be ten parts glad that I know so much! But your uncle will never know anything, for he gambles every night, so that he will never read a book, because every day he means to gamble again at night, and he is afraid of the word 'shü'!"

Ti stared at Yun. "It is not true!" he exclaimed indignantly, for his uncle had been quite kind and had gained the boy's love.

"Ask your uncle and see!" answered Yun tauntingly. "Does your uncle read a book any day? No, he gambles every night, and he is afraid of the word 'shü'!"

Ti stood and stared at Yun with great indignation. "My uncle is not afraid! My uncle is not a gambler!" he asserted, though he hardly knew what a gambler was, but guessed from Yun's words that it must be something discreditable.

Yun laughed. "You come from a little fishing-hamlet, and you know nothing!" said he scornfully. "You live in the same house with your uncle, and you do not know that he is a gambler! Ask him and see! Ask him to say the word 'shü'! He will not say it! Ask him! Every gambler fears the word 'shü'!"

Ti began to run. He wanted to get away from these taunting words. He did not believe them.

"Your uncle is afraid of reading a book!" Yun kept calling after him in Chinese. "Your uncle gambles every night, and he is afraid of the word 'shü'! I shall be much wiser than your uncle!"

Ti would not listen to anything more Yun said. He ran home to the store, feeling as if he did not want to go to see him again.

But alas! He found out that all Yun had said was true. His uncle was a great lover of gambling, and lost much money thereby. This was the reason why there often was not much money in the household, even though things in the store sold.

Now, Chinese gamblers do not like to read books before playing, because the word "shü," meaning "book," sounds like the word "shü," meaning "to lose," and these gamblers are superstitious. They are careful not to speak any word considered unlucky, lest such utterance should make them lose money when they play. Ti noticed that his uncle in speaking of the almanac — a useful thing by which a Chinese may compute the lucky or unlucky days and know when to commence any enterprise — never mentioned the almanac by its name, "t'ung shü," for there was that ill-omened word "shü" again. So he called the almanac "kat sing," or "lucky stars." Alas! As he gambled every night, there did not come a day when he would not have considered it unlucky to read the Jesus book, because it was a book, "shü." So he refused to read it, and was sometimes cross with Ti for asking.

One night, when he went out to play the gambling game of "Fán T'án," he took Ti, too, to the gambling place. There were no bright colors in the inner fán t'án cellar that the two entered through an outer cellar. There was white, the Chinese color of mourning, that makes players lose their money, and

TI: A STORY OF CHINATOWN.   39

the owners of the game gain the cash. There was a table covered with a mat,

The T'án Kún.

and there were some chairs. Other men secretly came in to play. Fán t'án games were forbidden by law in this city of the Americans, but little Ti did not know it. The two owners of the game, the T'án kún, or "Ruler of the Spreading Out," and the Ho kún, or cashier, were there. The T'án kún was a cross-looking Chinaman who stood by one side of the table, and the Ho kún was a crosser-looking Chinaman.

The stout door between this cellar and the outer portion of the cellar was barred.

Ti was very still. He felt sorry, for he knew it made his aunt angry to have his uncle lose money; and the teacher woman, after she learned that Ti knew his uncle gambled, told him that gambling was very, very bad. Ti thought the teacher was wise, and his aunt said so, too.

The players in the gambling cellar were still. It is not customary to talk while playing.

On the table there was a little pile of Chinese "cash," round coins with a square hole in the center of each piece. Ti looked on, while the T'án kún took a handful of cash and put them under a brass cup, and the players wagered their money on the numbers on the tin square, the "spreading out square," t'an ching, in the middle of the table.

Ti did not dare to say anything, everybody was so still. One Chinese player looked very downcast. On the way here, he had been jostled by somebody, and as

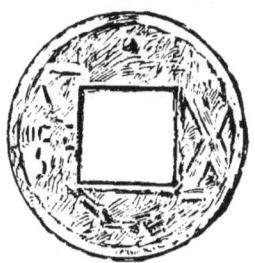

Chinese Round Cash.

that is an unlucky sign according to Chinese gamblers' superstition, he had turned back. But his desire to play fán t'án had brought him here at last, though he looked as if he expected to lose money.

Ti wished his uncle would come away from these men. He looked and saw that even the candles burning before the joss-shrine were white candles instead of red ones. There must be no color, excepting that which is supposed to be worn by the spirits of the dead.

Some time passed and yet the foolish Chinese players were eagerly absorbed in their game. They still placed their money beside the t'an ching in the center of the table, and the T'án kún counted the Chinese "cash" with the tapering rod of black wood used for this purpose. Over and over again the players wagered money, and Ti's uncle sometimes won and sometimes lost, but almost always lost. Some of the other men lost, too. Ti did not know that some of these Chinamen were employes in hotels, who sometimes in a single night lost all their money in fán t'án games or Chinese lotteries. But he was troubled because of what the teacher woman had said.

He slipped down on the floor and sat there, hiding his face. The eager players forgot him.

"My uncle is doing bad," thought Ti. "He gives all his money to the fán t'án men, and my aunt and the teacher woman are much sorry, and my uncle will never read the Jesus book, never! For he gambles every night, and he will not touch a book, and he is afraid of anything called 'shü.' So how will he ever read the Jesus book, as the teacher woman wished?"

The fán t'án game kept on in eager silence. Nobody thought of Ti, who crept under the table and went to sleep.

The next thing Ti knew, he was waked by a jar and a loud noise. There were blows on the outer cellar door, as if it would be broken in, and there were American men's voices in the other cellar. The lights of the cellar Ti was in were all out. Crash! came the blows of axes on this cellar's outer door.

"Uncle!" screamed Ti in Chinese.

Wide awake now, and frightened at the strange sounds, he scrambled from under the table, and stretched out his hands, expecting to feel somebody. He felt only empty chairs! Crash! crash! came the axes. The frightened little boy ran around the dark room, calling his uncle amid the tumult of sounds. He found nobody. He stumbled over an overturned chair and fell, hurting himself a little.

Ti lay where he had fallen, too frightened to rise. His heart beat so it gave him a feeling of suffocation.

"Uncle! uncle!" he cried.

Why were the lights all out? What did it all mean? Who was it that was trying to get in? Why had the Chinese all run away? Ti lay, a trembling, pitiful little object, in the dark. To his horror, the thick cellar door began to give out a splitting sound. He had faintly hoped that the door might be thick enough to keep the men out, whoever they were who were trying to get in.

He sprang up and ran wildly around in the dark, stretching out his hands and feeling no one to help him in his terror. He fell over chairs, he picked himself up, he cried out in fear. He did not know what was coming. There was so much noise that his voice was unheard by those men who were forcing their way in.

"Where is my uncle?" sobbed the scared child in Chinese.

The crashing and the sound of splintering wood was terrifying. The door was giving way.

"Bad men come in and catch me!" thought Ti, his heart thumping and a lump coming in his throat.

He found the table again and crawled under it. He waited, shivering. He did not know how to get out of the room. He and his uncle had come in by the now attacked door. In the dark the little boy could not see to escape. He could only crouch under the table, too frightened to attempt to search further for any passageway out of the room. There was not time. He must hide.

There was a great final crash. The stout cellar door gave way. Ti caught his breath. A flash of light illumined the dark room, and some men came in through the broken door.

It seemed to Ti that the men would see him the first thing. Oh, what would they do with him when they found him?

The frightened child shuddered. He had no doubt that he would be instantly killed.

CHAPTER VII.

THE OUTCOME FOR TI.

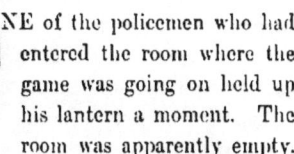

ONE of the policemen who had entered the room where the game was going on held up his lantern a moment. The room was apparently empty. No implements of fán t'án were visible. The players were gone. Nobody saw the little boy under the table.

"Stay by the door, Jim! They've run!" said one man hastily; and one policeman stayed, while the others ran through the cellar into the passageway.

Under the table, in the dark once more, Ti crouched and trembled. In a few minutes he heard distant blows as of axes again on wood. He could not understand what was happening. He did not know that when the policemen, who were making a raid on Chinatown fán t'án games, had followed the passage for a distance, they were suddenly confronted with some thick iron bars that crossed the passage and forbade further advance. When the Ho kún and the T'án kún and the excited players of fán t'án, alarmed over the police, had fled, forgetting Ti asleep under the table, they had escaped through these bars. There was a secret spring that the Ho kún and the T'án kún knew, and if this spring were touched, the iron bars would be raised out of the men's way and they could pass through, fleeing in haste from the police. But the bars had immediately been put in place again, and as the policemen did not know where the secret spring was, the only way they could go on in the passage was to chop down the posts to which the bars were attached. This took a little time, and the gamblers would have opportunity to conceal themselves or get out of the house by the many intricate passages.

The policemen at length chopped their way and went on, but they did not find what they sought. In some of the crowded little rooms of the building were Chinese quietly sitting, playing on little musical instruments such as the Chinese use, but no evidences of fán t'án or other games were in sight. Search as they might, the policemen could find nothing.

All this time, Ti was hiding under the table, back in the cellar. From under the table he peered fearfully out toward the dark, for he knew that one policeman was there. This one had no lantern. Everything was dark and the policeman kept so dreadfully quiet! Not a sound came from him. He was waiting, ready to catch any Chinaman, Ti knew. He was so afraid of that policeman! He did not know that a policeman might be the friend of a little Chinese boy who was not at all to blame for a fán t'án game, but had been brought here by his uncle. Poor little Ti! How scared he was!

After a while he heard the other policemen coming back to the cellar. They had given up their search in the farther rooms. They had found the Ho kún, and had recognized him as a man who was believed to know something about some fán t'án schemes, but there was no proof against him. So they could do nothing except order the Ho kún to go back to the cellar with them. If no evidences of fán t'án could be found there, the Ho kún would be unmolested further.

The policemen and the Ho kún re-entered the cellar. Ti crouched under the table.

"Why didn't somebody open the cellar door, then, when we first came?" a policeman was demanding of the Ho kún.

If Ti could have seen the Ho kún's face, the little boy might have noticed that it did not look nearly as animated as it had looked during the fán t'án game. The man had put on a very stupid and sleepy look.

"Why?" repeated the Ho kún sleepily. "Why? Keep door shut nights, evely night."

The police began to search among the chairs and about the room, but all the implements of fán t'án had vanished. Even the table's mat was gone. Where was the tin "spreading out square," "t'an ching," and the brass cup, "t'an koi," and the tapering black rod, "t'án pong"? Where was the "cash"? Ah! all these things had been caught up and run away with. The Ho kún felt sure that the police would never find the implements of fán

TI: A STORY OF CHINATOWN. 43

t'án where he had hidden them, and he remained tranquil, for he knew nothing to condemn him was in the cellar.

The policemen searched diligently and found nothing but Ti. It was a dreadful moment of discovery to the little boy. A policeman, seeing him under the table, drew him forth.

"Who's this?" he asked.

"Lil' boy," said the Ho kún blandly. "Nice lil' boy."

Ti burst into a loud wail of terror. The big policeman had children of his own at home. He did not want to scare this child.

"Well," said he, not unkindly, "you're in the wrong place, little chap. Don't cry, little fellow."

Then the policeman turned to the Ho kún. "What's your name?" he demanded.

"Wo Ki," answered the other, telling the truth, for of course "Ho kún" was only his official title as cashier of the fán t'án game.

"Well," said the policeman, "Wo Ki, I'd like to see you in jail, for I haven't the slightest doubt that you've had a fán t'án game running here. But if I can't find proof of it to-night, I know well enough you've had it; and let me warn you now, that if you don't quit such business, the first part of your name will come true!"

Wo Ki did not know exactly what that meant, since he was not familiar enough with the English word "woe" to know its similarity in sound to one of his names. Besides, what sounded as if it were Wo Ki's first name — according to American ideas — was in reality not his first but his surname, since Chinese put their surname first. It is as if one said "Smith Charlie" instead of Charlie Smith.

The police kept hunting, but the Ho kún assured them, "You look. You see. No fán t'án. Me no sabe fán t'án."

The Ho kún had never had any Christian training. All his life he had lived in heathen darkness. He did not speak the truth to the police about the fán t'án game.

But they did not believe his words. "Yes, you do sabe about fán t'án!" asserted one of them scornfully. "You know well enough about fán t'án! Didn't you hear about that Chinaman down at Los Angeles, who ran a fán t'án game, and was arrested, and had to put up two hundred dollars' bail?"

The Ho kún did not look as if he were aware what the word "bail" means. No one could look very much more stupid than he could when he tried.

The policemen were very loath to give up the search. They examined everything closely, hoping to find some secret place where the fán t'án implements might have been hidden. But the Ho kún and the T'án kún had known better than to hide such things in the cellar. Frightened Ti, crouching again underneath the table, cried silently, and dared not look out. But the policemen did not disturb him again. Ti could not understand all the English the policemen talked.

But the Ho kún was very sleepy and very stupid, until the policemen, giving up the search as useless, went out of the cellar door, through the outer cellar into the street, and away from the building. Then the Ho kún began to try to fasten the broken door as well as possible. Having finished, he turned to Ti, who was crouching trembling behind some chairs.

If Ti had been scared before in the presence of the policemen, he was almost more frightened now at being left alone with the Ho kún. He broke into sobs again. Where was his uncle?

"No cly! You come," said the Ho kún.

But the little boy fled. He rushed away from the Ho kún through the passage the police had traversed. No bars prevented him from running on, for the police had cut down the posts. Ti stumbled over them, though, on the floor. He sprang up again and ran. He wondered why he had not dared to run while the Ho kún was fixing the cellar door. He had been too alarmed to think of running, then.

The Ho kún followed through the winding way. Ti was beside himself with terror. He ran desperately through the dark, bumping into partitions. His heart was beating heavily. Oh, if he could only get away from this dreadful, following Ho kún! He wanted to cry so he could hardly keep down his sobs. A light was coming behind him. By it, before the Ho kún came in sight of the boy, Ti spied a little nook between two partitions. Trembling, he crowded himself into the narrow space and lay still.

On came the footsteps of the dreadful Ho kún. Ti held his breath. He was sure he would be found, and then what would become of him?

The light from the taper the Ho kún carried fell on his hardened face, as he hurried along the passageway. Ti's frightened eyes looked out at the man, who was calling. "Come! You come!"

The light was dim and the Ho kún did not see Ti in his nook. He hurried on, imagining the child was somewhere ahead. The little boy, left in the dark again, hardly dared breathe. The footsteps died away.

"He is walking softly," thought Ti. "He thinks he will find me and catch me. I am so afraid of him! He will come back when he does not find me. He will come back and find me here. I shall never see my father and my uncle and my aunt again. I am so afraid!"

He crawled out of the nook where he had hidden, and crept back along the passage. He wanted to go where the Ho kún would not come, wherever that might be.

In moving through the dark, Ti found a narrow passageway that turned off from the one by which he had come. He stumbled over some jars standing in the passage. He tried to hurry on, but it was of no use. The Ho kún, not having heard the child for a while, had been standing listening, and now came running back. He rushed down the passage and caught Ti, who screamed with terror.

But the Ho kún's big hand guided the little boy, by many queer, narrow passages, through to the other side of the building. There at a door opening into an alley, Ti's cowardly uncle who had run away from him, was waiting.

"No cly, no cly!" said the Ho kún; and Ti, seeing his uncle, tried to stop sobbing.

The uncle took Ti, and they slipped into the alley and hurried home. But when they reached the rooms above the back of his uncle's store, Ti cried all his frightened little heart out in his aunt's sympathizing arms. He did not want to stay in the city another minute! No, he wished to go straight back to his father and the fishing village. Oh, fán t'án was bad, bad, and there had been policemen!

The child wept and would not be comforted. He shrank from his uncle, who was so ashamed, or else so reluctant to lose the little fellow's confidence, that, going into the store, he got a pretty imitation red fish, made of cloth, and brought it back and gave it to him to wear with a crimson tassel as an ornament on the right-hand side of his blouse. The fish was pretty, but Ti could not recover from his fright. He cried himself to sleep, and during the next few days he kept begging so to be allowed to go back to the fishing-hamlet that his aunt and uncle were at a great loss how to make him contented to stay. They did not wish that he should go. They missed their own little children too much.

But now the teacher saw her opportunity to gain that which she had been refused before, though she had often requested it.

"If you will let Ti go to our school," she said, "he will see so many other little Chinese children that he will be happy and will not be lonesome. It will be much better for him than crying here at home and wishing he were at the fishing village. Do you not see it will? Won't you try it a while and see if we can't make Ti happy? The little children seem so happy and contented in our school."

The teacher dared speak longer and more urgently now than she had done heretofore, because she could see that Ti's uncle was in a humiliated frame of mind over his having frightened the child so badly. He had not intended that the visit to the fán t'án game should end so disastrously. How was he to have known that the police would choose that night for a raid? He well knew that Ti's father would have been angry to see his son in a fán t'án cellar. Ti might tell a woeful story to his father if he were allowed to go back to the fishing-hamlet just now.

Yet that other little boy who went to the teacher woman's school had not liked to put up incense sticks afterwards. That was the danger in sending children to the Christians' school.

Ti's uncle thought of this, but he reasoned that something must be done to keep the little boy more contented. Finally he said, "Yes, I let Ti go to school now," and the heart of the teacher was glad.

"Oh," she said to herself, "it was a good day when poor little Ti came from his fishing village down to this city! He is so bright. He will listen and learn to understand what we tell him, and will come to know Jesus for himself. If only we can have him a little while, and his father doesn't call him back to that fishing village, how much bright little Ti will learn!"

But Ti's aunt, Ah Cheng, did not know whether to be glad or sorry that he was going to attend the teacher woman's school. She thought about it a while, and then after the teacher was gone, she went to the old picture of the goddess of mercy, and poured out tea before the picture from the little teapot that was used for this purpose, and burned incense.

Yet even after worshiping, Aunt Ah Cheng went about her work troubled and afraid about the little boy's going to the teacher woman's school. She did not know how blessed a crisis in Ti's life this going to the Christians' school would prove to be.

CHAPTER VIII.

THE JESUS TEACHERS' SCHOOL.

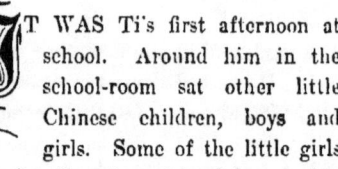

IT WAS Ti's first afternoon at school. Around him in the school-room sat other little Chinese children, boys and girls. Some of the little girls wore red, yellow-figured head-dresses that fitted over the upper part of the forehead and went around to the back of the head. These head-dresses had green borders and were somewhat like hats with the crowns cut out.

One little boy near him wore a cap with some Chinese words on the front of it. The words meant "Peace be with you in your going in and coming out." Another little boy wore a cap that said "Blessings" in Chinese. This boy had bracelets of jade on his chubby wrists, and one of the teachers came and asked him to take off the "Blessings" cap. The other little boy whose cap said the wish about peace had to take off his head-covering, too.

Most of the children in Ti's room were quite a little younger than he; so young that their heathen parents thought the children could not learn anything. But the children did learn. Some of the little ones sat on tiny low stools about a rectangular bin of sand, and played in the sand with long tin spoons. One chubby little Chinese girl, who lifted sand with a long spoon, could sing very well in her sweet baby voice a song that begins with

TI: A STORY OF CHINATOWN. 47

the words, "Up, up in the sky the little birds fly," and finishes with the words,

"Our heavenly Father, how kind and how good."

At some of the low tables sat other little girls with paper-weaving. One girl's queue was finished with braided pink and green and yellow and blue, and then wound on the back of her head so it looked like one of the flat table-mats that are sometimes woven by American children by aid of pins and thread of different colors. The Chinese children's blue and red colored shoes showed under the low tables. One little boy had read entirely through the First Chinese Book. It was a brown paper book with a red cover on one side, and Ti was determined that he would become as smart as that other little boy! He was glad, though, that he was to learn in this school instead of the one that Yun attended. He did not like to go with Yun any more, because

he kept speaking teasingly of his uncle's gambling.

Ti saw in the school-room before him a big chart with what he afterwards discovered was the Lord's Prayer in English, and on the walls were two strips of cloth, lettered with two texts written in Chinese and English. The texts were, "For God so loved the world, that he gave his only begotten Son, that whosoever believeth in him should not perish, but have everlasting life," and, "Believe on the Lord Jesus Christ, and thou shalt be saved."

Ti sat and listened as the children recited. He did not feel lonesome here or afraid. But how much the other Chinese children knew! The teacher — not the same one who had brought him to the school, but another with just as pleasant a face — stood before the children and asked in Chinese:

"Does Jesus love the little children?" and the children answered:

Ti did not know that these were words from the Jesus book, the book that his uncle would not read.

"What else does Jesus say?" asked the teacher; and the children answered:

"Come unto me, all ye that are weary and heavy laden, and I will give you rest."

Ti listened. Where had he heard those last words before? The other words that the children said were new, but somehow he seemed to remember something about those last words. He did not know what it was. He did not remember that those had been the words on the red paper he had given old See Yow at the fishing village.

"Suffer little children to come unto me."

TI: A STORY OF CHINATOWN. 49

But now the children sang, "Jesus loves me." Ti did not know what the teacher was thinking of, that she should look so sober while the children sang that song. But when the song was ended she told them that she was thinking of a little three-year-old Chinese girl who had been playing around in a missionary's study. The little girl hummed the words of "Jesus loves me" to herself. Then she stopped. "He don't love me!" said the child firmly to herself. "He don't! He don't!" The lady missionary overheard, and told the little Chinese girl that Jesus did love her. The little girl answered, "My mamma don't love him! She don't! She don't! She don't!"

The teacher said there were many Chinese parents who do not love Jesus. She wished all the boys and girls in her school might learn to love him while they were still children.

Ti heard a great deal of talk against the Jesus religion, at home, but he loved that teacher who had helped him when he was sick, and he listened very carefully to all that was said. Something told him that the Jesus teacher woman and such men as the T'án kún and the Ho kún were very far apart. He did not want his uncle to become such a man as the T'án kún or the Ho kún was.

In fact, on this first day of school, Ti received a good many new impressions, because the teacher did not have to talk to the children in English, but could explain things in Chinese. Yes, he heard a great many new things to-day.

When the teacher took the little boy home after school, she said to him, "Did you like school, Ti? Will you go to-morrow, again?"

Ti nodded, smiling.

The teacher's heart rejoiced. She

looked up at the tall building across the street in this Chinese quarter. She saw a Chinese boy angrily strike a child in a balcony. She saw an old Chinese man looking out of a window, a pipe in his mouth. She saw the dragon flag of China flying in

the breeze, with the emblems of one of the Chinese "tongs." High on one building there was a large sign in English words, though full of Chinese heathen meaning. The sign read:

```
CHOW LOON,
  4 FAMILY
  PARENTAL
TABLET SOCIETY.
```

And she thought of the light burning before the ancestral tablet in Ti's home, and in many other homes. And as she held the little boy's hand, she prayed in her heart that though he lived in darkness, yet that he might learn the truth.

"What did you learn to-day?" said his aunt to Ti, after the teacher had left him at home.

But the child could not tell what he had learned. He could not put his new impressions into words.

"You did not learn anything!" said his aunt.

"Nei kong tai wa," ("You do not speak the truth.") said Ti's uncle, who was at home and in a bad humor. "He has learned something and he will not tell us what it is! He will grow up to be like the Yesoo Yan!"

The "Yesoo Yan," or "Jesus man," was a Chinese shoemaker Ti's uncle knew. The shoemaker had become a Christian.

"His father will be very angry," went on the uncle crossly. "And I am angry! Ti shall not grow up to be like the Yesoo Yan! If he must go to that school, he shall go with me, too, wherever I will take him! Nei kong tai wa! He has learned something, and he will not tell us what it is!"

Ti tried to think what he had learned. But he found no words to express himself.

The uncle laughed, but looked at the little boy suspiciously. Who knew what the Jesus teachers had told him to-day?

"You shall go with me," he said, and the next afternoon he took Ti to a joss-house. The joss-house consisted of some rooms, reached by flight after flight of narrow, dirty stairs. Up and up climbed the child and his uncle till they came to the top story of the building. In a little ante-room sat the temple-keeper, who

TI: A STORY OF CHINATOWN.

sold the articles used in temple idol worship, such as candles, incense sticks, paper money, and paper clothes.

Ti's uncle bought of the temple-keeper an offering and the service of one of the temple-keeper's assistants.

Then the two proceeded to worship. The assistant beat on a drum to wake the gods. On a frame was hung a bell that the assistant might have used for the same purpose as the drum. There was a platform at the side of the wall in the joss-house, and six idols were waiting to be worshiped. The idols were of wood or plaster, and there was a glass lantern hanging in front of the gods, and in a box at their feet was sand, in which were small sticks of paper and sandalwood burning. There was also tea, ready made, in front of the gods.

In the Joss-house.

Ti's uncle sought the queer-shaped divining blocks, and threw them till they fell, one with its oval and the other with its flat side to the floor. This manner of falling was propitious. Then the sacred jar of bamboo splints was shaken till one splint fell to the floor. Each splint was numbered to correspond with numbers in the temple-keeper's book of prayers. The assistant, with a brush pen, took the number of Ti's uncle's splint and gave it to the temple-keeper, who in turn gave the answer according to the number.

About the walls and on the curtains were Chinese inscriptions in red and gilt and crimson. After making offerings and worshiping, the two went away from the crimson curtains and the images and the rows of brilliant banners and bronze fans, down the stairs again to the city street. The temple-keeper's assistant had lighted the paper money and carried it to burn in an oven kept for that purpose.

"You shall not grow up to be a Yesoo Yan!" said the uncle in Chinese to the little boy as they went home. "You shall grow up to worship the gods!"

Yet, because of his promise to the teacher, Ti's uncle did not forbid the little boy's going to the Christian school. He would not like to have the charge, "You do not speak the truth," applied to him. He had said that Ti might go, and the promise should not be broken. He took the child diligently to the Chinese joss-house on succeeding days, and one day, in a certain joss-house, he showed Ti a little side shrine for those dead Chinese persons who have no sons or other relatives in this world to offer prayers or incense in the dead persons' names. To this shrine charitable Chinese, who were not related to the dead, would come and lay offerings under the tablets that bore the names of the deceased persons. Otherwise the "wandering ghosts" of such persons are supposed to have no rest in the next world. Under some of the tablets bearing the names of women, at this shrine, Ti saw fans and jewelry such as a Chinese woman might use in this life.

The uncle kept the little boy long enough before this shrine to impress the child.

Before the Shrine.

"See," he said, "what would be, if you grow up to be a Jesus man! Your father has no other son. When your father dies, there will be nobody to burn incense for him, if you are a believer in the Jesus religion. You will leave your father to be prayed for at this shrine, and people will forget to do it. Yes, they will forget! You will leave your father all alone, all alone!"

The uncle's tone was very reproachful, and little Ti felt very sober. Surely he would never leave his father, his dear father, to be one of the poor, wandering, forgotten ghosts of the next world. He loved his father, and he went away from the joss-house thinking grave thoughts for so little a fellow. No wonder that some of the Chinese children shut their mouths tightly and shook their heads, when the teacher woman spoke about Jesus.

Yet, though Ti did not mean ever to neglect his father, the little boy could not disbelieve what the kind teacher said about Jesus loving little children. And he was afraid to go with his uncle to the joss-houses, for fear the uncle might on the way go to some gambling place, and he might again see the T'án kún or the Ho kún. It is very difficult to trust one's uncle entirely, after being once terrified by his acts. Ti would rather be with the teacher who had been so good to him when he was sick.

His uncle, however, was quite satisfied that he had greatly impressed the child.

"He will not be a Yesoo Yan," said the uncle to himself with a satisfied feeling of certainty. "No, he will not! He loves his father too well. I am glad I have showed him that shrine!"

And from that hour the vigilance of Ti's uncle began to relax. He did not know that despite what man may say or do in opposition, God's word, when faithfully taught, will have an effect. Ti was having very faithful, tender teaching in these days at the school.

And Ah Cheng, too, was beginning to think very differently. For when the teacher came each day to bring the boy to and from school, she often stopped to talk with Ah Cheng about Jesus.

CHAPTER IX.

TI'S TENTH BIRTHDAY.

I HAD been going to school for some time. The teacher came one day to take him there as usual. Her eyes were red. Ti could see that she had been crying. He wondered why. She looked as his aunt looked sometimes, when his uncle had thrown away all the money gambling and had come home cross and struck her.

He did not like to see anyone unhappy. The teacher, however, did not say anything about why she had been crying. She tried to control her trembling lips, and she did not talk about anything, all the time that Ti and she were going to school together.

When they came to the school-room, they found themselves quite early. The other scholars had not come yet.

Inside the school-room, Ti began to interest himself in some paper-folding that the children did. Suddenly, something made him look up, and he saw that the teacher was crying. He dropped the paper-folding, and ran to her and pulled at her sleeve.

"No cly," (cry) begged the little fellow gently. "Wha' fo' you cly?"

The teacher could not talk for a minute. Then she sat down, and Ti stood beside her, while she told him, partly in Chinese and partly in English, what had happened. He could understand a good deal of English now. The teacher told him that a poor Chinese girl who was brought to a mission Home had been dying of consumption, and she had said to a teacher, "I am dying. Stay with me." The sick girl could not understand English, but some other Chinese girls told her of Jesus and heaven. She had had a hard, sorrowful life, and now she listened and said that she would try to trust in Him. But after a while she said, "Oh, I am afraid I cannot understand the way." Then one of the Chinese girls prayed with her and tried to tell her how to talk to Jesus herself, so she might feel he was with her and wanted to comfort her. But the poor dying girl lay still a little while, and then said, "I am afraid the door of heaven will be shut. It will not open for me! I cannot see the way! Who will lead me?"

They prayed for her and told her Jesus would lead her to heaven and see that the door was open for her. After that she lay still for a time with closed eyes, then suddenly she opened her eyes, her face lit up with joy, and she cried, "I see the way! Jesus is with me and the door of heaven is open! It is all beautiful there! Oh, how beautiful!" and, almost instantly, she died.

"Oh, Ti!" said the teacher, as the tears ran down her face, "I am so glad the poor girl found Jesus before she died! She had had such a hard life, but when she heard of Jesus she believed, and I know she did find the gates of heaven open. But there are so many others that don't know about Jesus! Chinese girls and boys and women and men, Ti! I want you to know and love Jesus while you are a little boy. Won't you? So many Chinese don't know Jesus. We teachers do all we can, but we are so few, and there are so many to be told!"

The teacher bowed her head on her hands and sobbed. Then came the sound of the steps of other scholars, and she stopped crying, and turned to the little pupils.

But Ti's tender heart had been touched. He did not know that all that day there rang in the teacher's ears the words of that dying Chinese girl, "I am afraid the door of heaven will be shut. It will not open for me! I cannot see the way. Who will lead me?" To the teacher it was the cry of hundreds on hundreds of souls she was unable to reach. She felt as if her heart would break. She did not know that what she had said to one little Chinese boy this day would stay in his memory. She had said, "Oh, Ti, I want you to know and love Jesus while you are a little boy," and Ti's attentive heart had opened to that appeal.

He had been learning every day in the months he had attended this school. He no longer went home without being able to tell his aunt what he had learned. She asked him every day, and now he could tell her little texts he had learned in Chinese. Very short texts they were, but the aunt, as is often the way with Chinese women, believed more the word brought to her by childish lips than what the missionary woman had said.

One night when the aunt asked Ti the usual question, "What did you learn to-day?" he answered, "Honor father and mother," and she was much pleased that he had had such teaching in school, for the Chinese believe strongly in the honoring of fathers and mothers.

Ti's uncle had forgotten his first fear lest the little boy should grow up a believer in Jesus. He was absorbed in his own affairs, and he thought that the child was too young to learn very much at school, after all. So he let him go, without fear.

But Ti was learning more than either his uncle or his aunt guessed, although at home he of course had to see much heathenism, and one day, when the teacher called to take him to school, Ti was not at home. He was absent from school that day, because he had to go with his uncle and a number of Chinese men and women to the Chinese cemetery, out by the sand dunes near the ocean. They rode there in express wagons, which also carried provisions. Ti saw that the cemetery was divided by white fences into inclosures. His uncle told him that each inclosure was for a separate "tong," as the Ye On Tong, or the Tung San Tong. A small wooden altar was before each plot, and the provisions were taken from the wagons and laid on these altars. There were a number of whole, roasted pigs, decorated with colored papers and ribbons.

The Chinese bowed before the graves, and set off a good many firecrackers, and burned packages of colored papers, and the roast pigs standing on the altars soon looked out through air that was filled with smoke. Then the people went back to the city for a feast, since this was the twenty-fourth day of the second month of the Chinese year, the time of the Tsing Ming — "pure and resplendent" — festival, when the Chinese believe that the gates of the tomb are thrown open and the spirits of the dead are permitted to revisit the earth. Ti's aunt thought about her two little children, Whan and Hop, who had died, and she went to the cemetery with the other women and men. But though Ti did not know any better than to think it was right to make these many offerings at the graves, yet he did know and remember what the teacher woman had said about the gates of heaven opening for the sick girl, and his aunt cried when he told her.

The next day, when the teacher came to take the little boy to school, his aunt told why he had not been able to go the previous day. The teacher listened sadly. She knew how much of heathen customs surrounded the child. But Ah Cheng looked at the teacher at last and said hesitatingly, "Ti say the gates of heaven opened for the sick girl."

The teacher's heart rejoiced that the little lad had told his aunt.

"Yes, Ah Cheng, Ti is right. The gates opened for her, I am sure. She loved the Jesus who first loved us. And he loves the little ones."

These and many other words of comfort the teacher said that day as she lovingly talked with the mother.

"I am so glad we are keeping Ti so long!" thought the teacher joyfully. "So many parents take their boys out of school, but we are keeping him."

Ti himself had no intention of leaving the school. There was a class of older Chinese boys downstairs, and they had another teacher, and sang hymns in Chinese, and read Chinese books, and were very wise, Ti thought. Sometimes they sang in English, and one song they sang was, "Do you know what makes us happy? We are little friends of Jesus."

Ti could sing that song himself, and he meant it; only he never dared sing it where his uncle could hear.

The months slipped by till Ti was over nine years old. His father had several times wanted to take him back to the fishing village, but the uncle and the aunt begged to have him left with them, and the father reluctantly consented. So he stayed, and the Christian teaching went on.

Then there came a day that brought sad tidings to Ti. His father had been drowned in the bay, not far from the Chinese fishing-hamlet. He would never see his father alive again.

The little boy cried bitterly, for he loved his father. For a little while he was taken from school, and the teacher was very anxious, for she was afraid his uncle would never let him come back again. His mother had died several years ago, when he was quite small, and now he would probably live continually with his aunt and uncle, and the teacher knew that the uncle did not like the school.

But after a while, Ti came back to school with a sober little face and a small white cord, as an emblem of mourning, braided into his queue. The teacher knew that at his uncle's home the child was made to worship before the ancestral tablet, into which, according to Chinese belief, it was supposed that part of the spirit of Ti's father had entered. The

Chinese think that every spirit has three parts, one that goes with the body to the grave, one part that goes like vapor to heaven, and a third part that stays in the ancestral tablet. The teacher was sorry that Ti had to worship before the tablet on which his father's name was now written. She could not help it, but she tried to teach and comfort the little boy as well as she could.

"God grant that Ti may love Christ!" she prayed daily as the months went by. And at last she came to believe that her prayer was answered. She felt sure that, though Ti was a Chinese boy, he had really begun to know Jesus and was every day learning to love and trust him more, and that he was asking for help to do right.

Ti's tenth birthday came. He had learned very rapidly in school. He had long ago read through the First Chinese Book, and had been promoted to the more advanced room downstairs. He had learned and believed so much of gospel truth by this time that his uncle would have been much alarmed and very angry if he had known it. But the truth was, the uncle was becoming so inveterate a gambler that he had little thought or care for anything else. He was growing to smoke opium, also, and he was going down morally and intellectually. He did not know that for many months, now, Ti had been praying to Jesus. The little boy never put up the incense sticks before the idols, of his own accord, now, though his aunt wished to insist on his keeping up the ancestral worship. He tried to avoid doing that. Every few days mock-paper money and perhaps paper meant to represent clothing were burned before the ancestral tablet. It seemed to Aunt Ah Cheng a dreadful thing if Ti's father should be neglected now that he was dead! And the teacher knew that her little pupil was sometimes commanded to do things contrary to what she had taught him. One day Ti asked her if the gifts he offered could reach his father in the next world, and if it was true that his father's spirit was in the ancestral tablet.

"No, Ti, one of your father's spirits is not in the ancestral tablet. The Chinese are mistaken about that. But I am glad you love your father, who is gone, and think often of him; and Jesus is glad you love him. You cannot help him by offering gifts before the tablet, but you can talk to Jesus about your father, and he can comfort you and help you to do right in your home."

Ti listened, with his sober eyes intent on his teacher's, and she saw that the ten-year-old boy thought deeply. He avoided ancestral worship all he could.

"I am so glad Ti is growing up with us!" thought the teacher. "I hope we shall keep him. We have had him upwards of two years."

CHAPTER X.

TI DISAPPEARS.

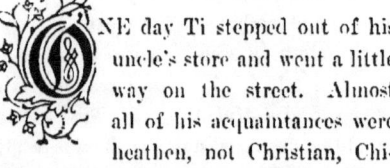NE day Ti stepped out of his uncle's store and went a little way on the street. Almost all of his acquaintances were heathen, not Christian, Chinese. He passed the old man who sat on a box on the sidewalk mending an opium pipe (jin ten), and passed also the other man who cobbled Chinese shoes on the sidewalk. He went across the street. There sat the fortune-teller behind his red-covered, ink-stained table as usual.

Ti was thinking of something he had heard lately at his mission Sunday-school about fortune-telling. The teacher had said that a fortune-teller could not know any more about what was going to happen in the future than other persons did. The fortunes he pretended to tell must be lies, and Ti knew that lying and deceit were wrong.

The fortune-teller had learned his business in China itself, and he considered himself an expert in his art when he remembered a blind fortune-teller who lived in China. Blind men there sometimes have this business, but they are under a disadvantage because they cannot read any Chinese book on the subject. There are several different ways of fortune-telling practiced among the persons of this business in China, and blind men have their own way. But Ti's city friend had a book on his table which told of a method that he pursued.

Ti went up to the fortune-teller's table. He was not doing any business just this moment, and he looked at Ti in a neighborly manner, as an American might look at a pleasant, well-behaved small boy who came in friendliness to stand and look at business. The Chinaman's future dinner, a tiny piece of fresh pork, with a bit of greens that had a yellow blossom like mustard, was in a brown paper cornucopia on the table, just as the fortune-teller had bought them of the Chinese butcher. His book was on the ink-stained red cover of the table, as were his writing pencil and a box.

"Have you gone to school to-day?" he asked in Chinese.

"Yes," answered Ti. "I go to school. Very good school. I read Chinese. I read my Chinese book. I read English book, too."

The fortune-teller looked at the little boy with approbation.

"It is very good to read Chinese and to have Chinese books," he said. "I have a Chinese book."

He laid his hand on the paper book of fortune-telling.

"You will be a great man," continued the fortune-teller to Ti. "Perhaps you will some day be a fortune-teller like me."

Ti looked sober. He remembered what he had heard at school. "No," said he, gravely, "I shall not be a fortune-teller.

The teacher woman says that no one can tell fortunes truly."

The man sat up angrily. "The teacher woman has an oily mouth and a heart like a razor!" he said angrily, using a proverb of the Chinese people. He meant that the teacher was a person who spoke pleasantly, but had a treacherous heart.

"May the Five Emperors catch the teacher woman!" he continued.

Ti shrank back. He had not supposed the man would be angry. The "Five Emperors" are certain five heathen gods that are believed by the Chinese to have power over pestilence, cholera, and so on. To say, "May the Five Emperors catch you!" is a Chinese malediction; therefore Ti did not like to have the man use it in speaking of the teacher.

The fortune-teller sat and scowled. Presently a customer engaged his attention. The customer paid his fee and went away. After this the man was more pleasant and talked, telling Ti of the fortune-tellers in China.

There came another customer. Ti looked at him. Then he wanted to run, for who was this second customer but the man who had been the Ho kún of the fán

The second customer was the Ho kún.

t'án game to which his uncle had taken him on the evening when the police made their raid.

Ti shrank back, but the Ho kún did not seem to recognize him. The child stood there, not daring to run lest he should draw to himself the attention of this dreaded person.

The Ho kún wanted the fortune-teller to discover whether the twenty-fifth day of the month would be a lucky day for him to do something. What the something was, Ti did not understand. The Ho kún was beginning to explain about it, when the fortune-teller suddenly caught him by the sleeve of his "shom" (blouse) and hurriedly said something warning but unintelligible to Ti.

The Ho kún evidently took the warning, whatever it was. Then the fortune-teller proceeded to open his box of small, folded papers. Inside each folded paper was written a Chinese character. The fortune-teller told the Ho kún to choose two papers. This he proceeded to do at random, one at a time. Then the fortune-teller took the two chosen papers, opened them, and saw what the Chinese characters were. Now Chinese characters are made up of different parts. The fortune-teller, according to the rules that he usually followed, divided the two chosen characters into their separate, distinct parts. Afterwards he asked the Ho kún some questions in so low a tone that Ti, who stood at one side, did not understand. He was not trying to understand, anyhow. His one great anxiety was that the dreadful Ho kún should go away.

The fortune-teller, by some adroit strokes of his writing pencil, made some new words out of the parts of the Chinese characters, and then gave his opinion. It was that the twenty-fifth day of the present Chinese month was a most unlucky day for the Ho kún. Days that are lucky for one person are not always lucky for another, according to Chinese belief, but the twenty-fifth day of the present month would be the unluckiest kind of a day for the Ho kún to do what he intended to do. The fortune-teller emphatically charged him to put off doing it till the fifth day of the next month. That would be a lucky day for him.

Ti heard so much, but he did not understand, any more than before, what the Ho kún's undertaking was.

"Do it the fifth day of next month!" charged the fortune-teller again and again; and the Ho kún, duly impressed, promised, paid his money and went away.

The fortune-teller looked at Ti. For an instant the little boy thought that he was almost sorry about something.

"You like me tell your fortune?" inquired he.

Ti shook his head and smiled.

"Good-by," he said in English; and he hurried away across the street to the safety of his uncle's store.

He did not know that the fortune-teller stood and watched him cross the street and then muttered, "The fifth day of the next month will be lucky for the Ho kún!"

What the Ho kún had come to consult the fortune-teller about was this: Ti's uncle, through his gambling and through borrowing, had become greatly in debt to the Ho kún, so much in debt as to almost equal the value of his store. The T'án kún and the Ho kún, finding that he made no payments, knew enough of American customs to resolve to put an attachment on the little store. Ti's uncle had really lost everything. Yet the Ho kún was enough of a Chinaman to want to consult a fortune-teller about which day would be the fortunate one on which to attach the store. As Ti had been present, the fortune-teller had warned the Ho kún not to explain aloud what he intended to do.

Ti went home, ignorant that the future plans of the Ho kún would affect his future. And the fortune-teller stood and looked, and muttered in Chinese again to himself, "The fifth day of the next month will be a lucky day for the Ho kún!"

But the fortune-teller had a plan of his own, and it was because of this hastily-conceived plan to help Ti's folks a little, that he had charged the Ho kún again and again that the twenty-fifth day was unlucky. The twenty-fifth day of the present month would be to-morrow, but the fifth day of the next month would give a little time for the fortune-teller's plan.

Ti was now so large that for some time he had been going to the American teacher's school and returning home again daily, without the teacher being obliged to go and come with him. He knew the way and felt quite safe.

But the fifth day of the next Chinese month the teacher looked very much worried. Ti was not in school. He had not been there the day before, either, which was Monday. She had not seen him since Friday in school.

"I will go around that way just as soon as school is over to-day," she thought anxiously. "There must be something the matter. I meant to have gone last night, as he wasn't at school yesterday. But I had so much to do."

Immediately after school she went to Ti's home. She was startled when she went in. The door at the head of the outside stairway had been unfastened, and after her customary knock she opened the door as usual. But the room was empty. No one was visible to tell what had happened.

"Why, I wonder if they've moved?" said the teacher to herself.

A new, forbidding-looking woman lifted a red curtain that hung before the doorway of a room, and the teacher appealed to this stranger.

"Where have the folks gone?" she asked in Chinese. "The little boy gone? All gone?"

The woman only stared at her and did not answer. She repeated her question, but the woman did not return a word.

"Perhaps I can find out down in the store," thought the teacher.

She went down the outside stairs and around to the front of what had been Ti's uncle's store. There she was disturbed to see new faces. Ti and his uncle and aunt were not there. A Chinaman with a hard face scowled at her from behind the counter.

"Where is Ti? Where have they all gone?" she asked anxiously.

The Chinaman shook his head sullenly.

"Don't you know?" she asked.

The Chinaman shook his head and scowled harder. He was the man who had been Ho kún in the fán t'án game in the gambling cellar, but of course the teacher did not know this.

"Have they moved?" she asked.

"They all go 'way! Never come back any more!" was all the Ho kún would say.

The troubled woman turned and went out of the store. The instant she appeared the boy Yun, the son of the Chinese newspaper man across the street, came running over toward her.

"Teacher woman," asked Yun eagerly, "you like know where Ti gone?"

"Yes," answered the teacher quickly. "Where is he gone? What's happened?"

"Ti's uncle gamble, gamble all the time," explained Yun in English. "Get gleat debt to Ho kún man! Ti's uncle take Ti and his aunt and go 'way off to China on China steamer this morning! Never come back to Cal'forn'a any more! They go on China steamer this morning!"

"Gone to China!" exclaimed the startled teacher.

She knew a steamer had really started for China that morning. It was steamer day.

Yun nodded. "They go China this morning!" he said.

For an instant the teacher was overwhelmed. Then she recollected that no Chinaman who was in debt could go to China without first paying his creditors, and Yun had just said that Ti's uncle had been in debt to the Ho kún.

"How could Ti's uncle go if he owed the Ho kún man?" asked the teacher. "Every steamer day the ship agent stands one side the gang-plank to take steamer tickets, and the Six Chinese Companies' man stands the other side to take each Chinaman's release ticket, showing he has paid his obligations to the company that represents his province in Canton. Ti's uncle couldn't leave America without that release ticket. The Six Companies wouldn't allow it. He must have paid his debts to the Ho kún man somehow, or he can't have gone."

Yun stood silent. The teacher looked gravely at him.

"Oh," she said suddenly, "I see now how it was! Those Chinamen who have the store now must have bought it, and so Ti's uncle had money to pay his debts; or else the Chinamen took the store instead of his paying them. Perhaps that was the way he got out of debt and could go to China."

"Yes," said Yun readily, "they go to China this morning on steamer."

The teacher had no doubt of the story now. Ti's folks had gone to China. And the little boy was gone!

Her face was pale and startled as she stood there. She did not know this was a lie that the Chinese fortune-teller, who had a grudge against her because she did not approve of his business, had sent Yun to tell. The fortune-teller knew the teacher would feel badly over Ti's going so far away as China. Yun did not really knew where he had gone. He suspected he was telling a lie, but he thought it was well to obey the fortune-teller, and, brought up in a heathen home, he had little scruple about telling the teacher a lie.

"They must have kept it a secret from Ti until the very last that he and they were going to China," said the teacher. "He could not have known it, or he would have told me in school last week. This is Tuesday, and he was not at school yesterday. I have not seen him since Friday. If he had known then that he was going away, he would have said good-by to me. Gone to China! Poor little Ti!"

She did not doubt the story, for she had seen other scholars vanish as summarily from her school. But she had so hoped to keep Ti! She felt stunned, overwhelmed, as she turned away. She did not know that the fortune-teller was watching. Yun went away.

"Probably Ti's uncle was afraid I would say some last words about Jesus that the child would remember," she thought. "The uncle and aunt didn't want me to know he was going."

The teacher looked blankly at the Chinese red papers and great lanterns. She saw afar the table of the apparently oblivious fortune-teller. Then she did not see anything clearly, because of the rush of tears that blinded her. It seemed as if the great sea of heathenism had risen and swept away bright, loving, studious Ti. She remembered the joss-house of the "Queen of Heaven" on the next street. But oh, with all the heathenism of this Chinese quarter, how much darker was China itself! And Ti was on the way there, perhaps never again to hear a word about Christ! What would become of him, little Ti, who had grown so dear to his teachers and had seemed to open his heart so readily to Christianity? Here, Christians could penetrate Chinatown. In China there might not be a Christian or a missionary that he could see!

"Oh, my little scholar! My little Ti!" she cried. "I can't help you any more! I'm afraid I sha'n't ever see you again! Oh, God keep you, in the world of heathenism! God help you not to forget Jesus! Oh, dear little Ti, God keep you!"

With sorrowful heart the teacher went away. She could only ask God to care for Ti wherever he was.

The teacher, however, had been greatly deceived as to Ti's present whereabouts. He was not going to China at all. What had happened really was this: The evening of the day on which the fortune-teller had been consulted by the Ho kún as to the luckiness or unluckiness of the twenty-fifth day for putting an attachment on Ti's uncle's store, the fortune-teller ate his supper as usual, and then in the darkness secretly wended his way to see Ti's uncle. He did not usually tell the secrets intrusted to him by customers, but he liked Ti and was not unwilling to help his folks a little.

Ti's uncle was ignorant of the fact that any attachment was to be placed on his store. This evening the fortune-teller told him just what the Ho kún intended to do on the fifth of next month. The fortune-teller could not help him by letting him have money, but he suggested that if there was anything special that he would like to save before that attachment was put on his store, he would do well to save it before the fifth of next month.

Ti's uncle was greatly excited over the bad news. He did not know how he could get any money to pay the Ho kún, for the amount needed was large. The fortune-teller said that the reason he had told the Ho kún to wait till the fifth of next month was because he knew that was the day a steamer sailed for China, and he also knew that the junk from the Chinese fishing village up the bay would probably come down to the city the third or fourth day of the month, as there were one or two Chinese from the fishing-hamlet who wanted to go to China the fifth day. He suggested to the uncle that the best way would be to send his wife and Ti back to the fishing village by the junk, and they could carry whatever valuables could be saved from the store. The main contents of the store could not be saved without a wagon's coming, and the Chinese neighbors' finding out what was going on, and the Ho kún's probably being told and his rushing in and defeating the plan. The Ho kún would not probably wait for the fifth day in that case. So the store must go. But, if he did not suspect anything, he would not put on the attachment till the fifth day of the month, and meantime Ti's uncle might secretly save something.

"You keep still! Don't tell the neighbors you are going! Don't tell Ti!" warned the fortune-teller in Chinese. "He might tell his teacher! You keep still! When junk comes, you have things ready and you go quick at night when nobody see!"

This plan was carried out. Ti's uncle watched for the junk. The third evening of the next month, greatly excited, he hurried back from the wharves to tell his folks the junk had come. That was the first Ti knew about the plan of moving. None of the neighbors knew. Secretly in the dark Ti's uncle hurried such things to the junk as he could carry. He returned, hurried Ah Cheng and the little boy out in the evening darkness, and hastened to the wharves. It was a breathless hour, for he knew he was saving some things that the Ho kún expected to put an attachment upon.

Ah Cheng and Ti and the bundles reached the junk, and Ti's uncle breathed more freely. He stayed on board that night. The junk, having delivered at the city the passengers who expected to go to China the fifth, would now sail back to the Chinese fishing-hamlet the next morning, the morning of the fourth, not waiting till the China steamer sailed.

Ti's uncle would not go to the fishing-hamlet. He would stay behind in the city. He hoped to go to China in some way, after he had given up the store to satisfy his creditors. He could not go by this steamer, for he must earn his passage money yet, and satisfy two other creditors for small sums before he could go. But he had been wanting to go to see his old father and mother, and now would leave Ti and Ah Cheng with the other uncle, Lum Lee, and his folks at the Chinese fishing village.

In this hurried, breathless going, there had been no time for Ti to send any good-by to his teacher at the mission school. He felt very badly.

"Teacher woman not know where I go," the boy told his uncle. "She feel bad."

At last, when his uncle was leaving the junk, early in the morning just before it sailed, Ti begged so hard that the uncle would tell the teacher where he had gone and why he could never come to her school again, that the uncle promised.

"Yes," he said, "I tell the teacher woman. I tell her to-day."

So the junk sailed away on its course and the uncle went back to his store. He had no intention of telling the teacher anything. He had only promised in order to make Ti stop begging. Neither had he any intention of telling any one where his wife and Ti had gone. As soon as the Ho kún and the T'án kún put the attachment on the store the fifth day of the month, Ti's uncle vanished. The T'án kún and the Ho kún took possession, and the teacher received no information from the uncle about the little boy's destination.

In the succeeding days the teacher fully believed that Ti had gone to China. As a matter of fact, not even his uncle had gone to China yet, for he was partially engaged in opium smoking, to help him forget the mortifying fact of his having lost his store, and he was also partly occupied with plans for earning his passage money to China. He did not go near his former store, so the teacher never met him.

CHAPTER XI.

TI IS TESTED.

ONE day, a while after Ti's going away, the teacher was startled. With some other Christian workers she was out on an errand of mercy among the tenements of Chinatown. They had not found the Chinese person they sought. They went further, down a long, narrow alley, on either side of which were fish and vegetable stalls. The sidewalks were so narrow that the little party walked in the center of the alley, on the cobblestones. They opened one door of the alley, and, as they shut that door behind them, they passed into utter darkness inside of a building. They found their way up one flight of stairs. At the landing, all was darkness. They groped to the right and went up another flight of dark stairs. They stumbled through narrow black passages. Here and there were little rooms like cupboards. In these tiny rooms on shelves Chinamen lay.

"We've found an opium joint!" whispered one of the men of the party.

It was so. In the blackness of the little cupboard-like rooms the only light would be that coming from a wick burning in a tumbler and illuminating the smoker's face. By the light could be seen the nut-oil lamp (the dong) for cooking the opium, the bamboo pipe (jin ten), and the needle for manipulating the opium (ah pin yin).

The visitors, intent on the object of their search, hurried past these closet-like rooms. They stumbled in the dark, wishing they had thought to bring a lantern, for though it was daylight in the alley, it was like night here.

At length the party found a woman who assured them that the one they searched for could surely be found in another house in another part of Chinatown. The informant seemed honest, and there was nothing to be done but for them to retrace their steps through the dark hallways.

They had reached the back of the building. "Look down," murmured one of the party. Below, in the narrow yard between this building and the next, there arose a cloud of steam. "It's the opium factory!"

The very yard below was somewhat dim, for besides its narrowness and its situation between the two tenements, it was boarded at either end, and, above, the roofs nearly formed a covering. The party looked down as well as they could, and perceived, in the narrow yard, a place built of cement, in which were furnaces for charcoal. There was the sight of the steam of boiling opium and a glimpse now and then of the charcoal's red glow. Two scantily-dressed Chinese coolies were kneading opium, as the water evaporated, in brass dishes that were over the furnaces. The coolies were strong men, for opium-kneading requires considerable strength.

"The opium becomes more and more stiff, so that it's harder to knead," softly said one of the party. "At the right time those coolies will use brass flatteners to form the opium into a thick cake at the bottom of each dish. Then the dishes will be turned upside down over the embers, and the men will lift the cakes every minute, and peel off the skin that has cooked. So each opium pancake will make fourteen or fifteen thinner ones."

TI: A STORY OF CHINATOWN. 67

The party did not linger, but stumbled back through corridors and black stairways, trying to find the way to the alley once more. They began to go by other little cupboards with shelves covered with matting. Lying, getting ready to smoke, on one shelf was a young Chinaman, who seemed to be somewhat ashamed, and explained aloud to the party of strangers that he only smoked "one li gee of opium a day." One li gee is twenty cents' worth.

They hurried on in the blackness. Suddenly, as they passed one of the black little cupboards, a Chinese face dimly lit by the light from the dong shone from the darkness. The teacher gave a little cry and caught the arm of the next one in her party.

"Wait a minute! Wait!" she exclaimed. "I must speak to this opium smoker. I think I know him. I want to ask him a question. I thought he was in China. I thought he had taken his folks there."

The party stopped. They knew the teacher must have some particular reason for her request. Out of the blackness of the weird little smoking-room, the yellow light from the dong made the Chinese head the more striking as one looked at it, the only visible thing amid the heavy shadows.

The Chinaman had not appeared to notice the party at all.

"You are Ti's uncle, are you not?" asked the teacher clearly in Chinese.

"Where has Ti gone? Has he gone to China?"

There was no reply. The sallow, half-narcotized face stood out of the blackness, but there was no look of recognition, no apparent realization that he had been addressed. The opium had done its work.

"He is too stupid to understand," said one of the party in English.

The man's head, resting on a wooden pillow, did not stir. The teacher knew, however, as she looked, that she was not mistaken. It was Ti's uncle who lay there.

"Where is Ti?" she repeated more loudly in Chinese. "I am the teacher woman. You remember me! I was at your house when little Hop died. I have been there many times. Where is Ti? Tell me, where is Ti now?"

The yellow face, surrounded by the heavy black shadows, did not open its lips to reply.

It seemed to the teacher as if she could not give up without any answer. She was startled and excited over finding Ti's uncle. Could it be possible that the little boy was still somewhere in this great city? If only she could find and help him!

"Just let me try once more," she begged her party in English. She turned to Ti's uncle again, and took up Chinese speech.

"Won't you tell me where Ti is?" she begged. "Only tell me this one thing.

TI: A STORY OF CHINATOWN.

Is he in this city? Tell me, yes or no! Is he here?"

She waited. There was no response. It was not the silence of refusal, but of stupidity.

"It's too bad, but you can't make him comprehend your question," said one of the party; and the teacher knew that it was so.

There was no use in waiting any longer. The little company went on, carrying the remembrance of the vision of that one yellow face in the blackness. The visitors groped out of the passage-ways through the door at last into the light of the alley again.

And this was the teacher's first clew to Ti's whereabouts. It was a very slender clew. She knew no more than before where the uncle had sent the little boy. Certainly he was not in that opium factory, she thought.

But the fact that she had seen Ti's uncle made the teacher, for the first time, doubt the story that Yun had told about Ti's going to China. She had supposed that he told the truth. Now she began to look for her little pupil daily, as she went about her busy work of visiting the Chinese women and children in their homes. She believed that Ah Cheng and Ti must be in the city, too, as long as the uncle was.

"I think Ti will keep on praying as we taught him," she told herself. "And yet, I wish I could be quite sure!"

Ah! it is so hard sometimes, after sowing the seed patiently, to have no opportunity to care for and cultivate it!

The teacher watched and sought in vain for some time, without gaining the slightest trace of her little pupil. Then once more she thought she had found a slight clew.

It was on the departure of a steamer for China. The teacher had gone to the wharves to see a Christian Chinese family and say good-by to them as they started for the old home in China again.

It was almost time for the vessel to sail. The wharf was full of people, white and Chinese. Coolies hurried over the gang-plank. Some Chinese carried their belongings wrapped in matting; some had baskets or sheets or boxes. All was bustle and hurry. There was a laugh at one Chinaman, who had dropped his box on the wharf. The box had broken open, and his goods had flown hither and thither. He hastily gathered his belongings. He had clothing, and dried herbs, and a box of huge pills. Hurriedly he crammed the things into his box again, and fled toward the gang-plank of the steamer, which was almost ready to lift.

The teacher had just come off the steamer, where she had been bidding the Christian Chinese family God-speed. As she stepped off the gang-plank to the wharf, the Chinaman who had so hastily gathered his belongings rushed past her. She had only one glimpse of his face as he ran by, but she knew him. It was Ti's uncle.

TI: A STORY OF CHINATOWN. 69

With a cry she sprang back, but it was too late. The Chinaman ran on the vessel. The gang-plank lifted. The water was covered with bits of papers, being prayers thrown by Chinese on the dock for the safe return home of the voyagers. She called across the water, but Ti's uncle did not look behind him. He plunged inside the vessel, out of sight.

"Oh," she cried, "can Ti be on board, too, and his aunt? They were not with the uncle! Is he going to China alone, or are they on board, too? If only I could have seen my little pupil! If only I had known, when I was on board, I'd have hunted the vessel over! I did look, but I didn't expect he was there. Is he?"

The steamer swung around. The teacher looked eagerly at the crowd on the decks. People were waving farewell. The width of water between the wharf and the steamer grew greater. She drew a long breath.

"Oh, my Ti!" she said, as she watched the steamer, "may God keep you, even though you go where there is no one to teach you any more about Christ!"

Away from the great city, in the little fishing-hamlet far up the bay, the old red paper still showed its message to the Chinese fisher-people as they passed along the narrow, crooked street. But none of the passers-by paid any attention to it. There were various red or yellow or white papers about the doors of other hovels, but when the papers were renewed, See Yow had always saved Ti's red paper with its "new words."

In the one street Chinese men and women were as busy as they had been two years before, when Ti had gone away.

See Yow.

Now, out on the rocks, a boy was turning some fish. By and by he had the numerous little fish all turned, and he left the rocks and went away, through the narrow street, past the little houses, to the place where old See Yow used to live. See Yow was ill, now, and he had been put into a sort of rude shed back of the small hut he and half a dozen other Chinamen had occupied. Poor old See Yow! He had not been able to walk to the shrine for a long time.

To-day he felt so feeble that he did not open his eyes when the boy entered the shed. Ti - - for the boy was Ti — went out again, and cooked some rice, and brought it to the old man. But he could take little.

The boy sat down at his side. See Yow lay still for a little while. Presently he stirred and said in Chinese, "Tell me the new words."

And Ti, who knew he meant the words on the red paper outside the door of his former hut, repeated the "new words" in Chinese: "Come unto me, all ye that labor and are heavy laden, and I will give you rest."

"Tell me again what the teacher said about the 'new words.'"

Ti straightened, and before he began to speak, thought hard as to all the teacher had tried to make him understand.

"She said," he began, "that when Jesus lived here on earth, folks who were in trouble came to him and he helped them; and that when they are tired or sick now, they can tell Jesus about it, and he will help them to bear trouble and sickness, 'cause he is never far away, but close beside us."

"But," said See Yow, interrupting, "how can one come to him, as the new words say?"

"When we love folks, we trust them. And though we cannot see this Jesus, he is with us. He has helped me, just little Ti. He makes my heart glad, for I know he loves me — and I love him, too." This last the boy said very softly.

There was silence. Old See Yow breathed heavily, but he was awake.

Then Ti began to sing. It was a song with Chinese words, but it told how Jesus had come down from heaven to show people how much he loved them and wanted to help them, and that he would take them to live with him in heaven, if only they would believe on him. It told how he even died to show his love. It was a song that Ti had learned in the little mission school in the city. It had very easy words and its meaning was very plain, so that a little child might understand. Oh, teacher in that mission school in the city, you knew not what you did when you taught Ti that song and the meaning of the "new words"! You knew no more than did the other teacher who years before had sent the red paper to Ti at the fishing-hamlet, as to what would be the result of your act. But the Lord of the harvest takes care of seed sown for him.

By and by Ti left Sea Yow, to attend to some more fish.

The little boy met his aunt, Ah Cheng, outside in the street, carrying some salt for the shrimp-curing. Ti and Ah Cheng had to work quite hard, now, for Uncle Lum Lee always expected anybody who lived with his family to work. Uncle Lum Lee was very fond of money; he and his wife worked hard, and saved all they could. Ah Cheng and Ti were perfectly willing to work, however, and as Ah Cheng's opium-smoking, gambling husband was not present to make the days wretched with his crossness and his blows, they were not very unhappy, though often very tired. In one thing Ah Cheng could already see that there was going to be trouble, however. Ti was neglecting ancestral worship and did not bow to the gods. She felt worried, though she had not said anything about it to Uncle Lum Lee's folks. Ah Cheng had not learned to believe in Jesus as Ti did, and Uncle Lum Lee's wife was a firm believer in the gods.

Uncle Lum Lee prized the shrines of the fishing village as being places where, according to his thinking, he could discover which were the luckiest days to go fishing. Still Ti, young as he was, noticed that the shrines did not seem always to give correct information, even on that subject. He did not dare, however, to say anything about it. He was glad to have been let alone, thus far, and not have the "Jesus book" discovered and taken from him. Though he could not read the Jesus book perfectly, yet he could read it somewhat, and he prized it. Uncle Lum Lee's folks did not know that he possessed it.

Ti smiled at his aunt now, and hurried away to attend to his fish. The aunt went on with her salt.

Back in the little shed, old See Yow, weak and sick, lay still. His withered, wrinkled face was very thin.

By and by, with an effort, the old man raised himself on his elbow. He looked cautiously around the interior of the shed, as if to make sure that no one but himself was in the little room. Then he lay back and shut his eyes, as he had seen Ti do when he prayed.

"Jesus," murmured old See Yow almost inaudibly in Chinese, " Jesus Christ, I am only a poor old fisherman Chinaman. I have heard the new words. Jesus Christ, I never heard them when I was young. I have heard the new words now when I am old, a very poor old fisherman Chinaman. Jesus Christ, make the center of my heart understand the new words before I die!"

Slowly, over and over, with pauses for breath, the old man repeated his prayer.

Out by the long tables for fish-drying, back of the hamlet, Ti worked. Once he looked up, and the sunlight glittering far on the bay struck his eyes, and the boy thought of his father who had been drowned out in that stretch of waters. The lad's face grew very wistful as he worked. He did so wish that he could have told his father what the teacher taught at the mission school, and could have sung to his father that song about Jesus loving everyone. But just as he was thinking this, Uncle Lum Lee came by. He was in a surly mood.

"Work harder!" he said sharply to Ti in Chinese, though the boy was already working as faithfully as anybody could.

Ti redoubled his efforts, while his uncle frowned.

Uncle Lum Lee was becoming very suspicious of Ti. From various things he had observed in him, he was coming to believe that the boy had had altogether too much teaching in that Christian mission school in the city. This money-loving Chinaman thoroughly despised the unbusiness-like way in which Ah Cheng's husband had lost his store, and he also thought that allowing Ti to go so long — two years — to the teacher of the "Jesus doctrine" was another wrong thing in Ah Cheng's husband.

Uncle Lum Lee had not been very diligent himself about worshiping the gods sometimes, but he despised Christians. He knew the Chinese saying, sometimes written over temple doors in China. "Worship the gods as if they were present." Sometimes he had doubted if they were present, but he had remembered the common saying of China, "It is better to believe that the gods exist than to believe that they do not exist." So he had gone on carelessly performing the usual rites; but now, roused by the thought of what he suspected in Ti, his zeal for the Chinese gods was reviving daily. Angry indeed would he have been if he had known that a few moments before this Ti had been singing that little mission song about Jesus to old See Yow in the shed. But everybody had been away, busy about the fish and the shrimp-curing, and nobody but old See Yow had heard the song.

"Go, put salt on the shrimps!" said Uncle Lum Lee now, giving Ti a rough push: and the boy went obediently.

All continued well until evening. Ti, having finished his work, was going to his uncle's hut to eat supper. On the way he met his uncle.

"Go worship Poo Saat!" said Uncle Lum Lee sternly.

Ti did not answer. There was something in his uncle's face that frightened the boy. He hesitated, trembling. His uncle gave him a push and went on, but Ti knew he was watched.

CHAPTER XII.

TI IS NOT HAPPY.

IT WAS the first time that Ti had been commanded to worship the gods. He turned and went toward the building where the sails and tackle belonging to the junk and other vessels of the fishing-hamlet were kept. Going into the building, he was face to face with the idol Poo Saat, revered by his uncle. Incense sticks were there. Ti stood in the middle of the sail-room, and looked at the idol. Then he looked at the incense sticks. Should he set up new ones and burn them? What was that verse the teacher had taught him in the little school in the city?

"Little children, keep yourselves from idols."

There was another verse: "We know that there is none other God but one."

How many times Ti had recited those verses with the other Chinese boys in the teacher woman's school! But oh, the words had not meant to him then nearly as much as they meant at this moment! What would Uncle Lum Lee do if he did not worship?

"Little children, keep yourselves from idols."

Ti stood and looked at the idol Poo Saat. Then he sat down on a coil of rope.

"I will not put up incense sticks to Poo Saat," thought he. "I will not worship him. If my uncle does not see me for a little while, he will think I have been worshiping Poo Saat. I will not worship, but I will sit here a little while. How can my uncle know?"

Then he began to feel troubled. Was it right for a boy who believed in Jesus to let any one think he worshiped Poo Saat?

Suddenly he started. There was the sound of feet coming to the sail-room. He jumped up as Uncle Lum Lee came into the room. The uncle looked at Ti, and the little boy trembled, so stern was that look.

"Why do you not worship?" asked Lum Lee in Chinese.

His tone was a very angry one. He took some incense sticks and ordered Ti to place them before the idol.

The boy took the incense sticks. He stepped toward Poo Saat. "I must do it!" thought he. "My uncle will strike me. He will strike me very hard. He is so angry!"

Then suddenly there swept over him the thought of Jesus. He seemed to see the teacher's face as she had pleaded with him that time in the school-room. "Oh, Ti, I want you to love Jesus while you are a little boy. Won't you?" He could see her as she had told him of Christ's love for him. And now he, Ti, was going to put these incense sticks before Poo Saat, and bow down and worship! He was going to do this because he was afraid. Afraid! — and Jesus loved him! Jesus died for him, poor, sinful Ti!

The great tears welled up in the boy's eyes till he could hardly see the idol. With a great sob, he threw the incense sticks from him. He flung himself down on a coil of rope and sobbed aloud. He could not worship Poo Saat!

"Little children, keep yourselves from idols," he sobbed in Chinese.

For an instant Uncle Lum Lee stood and looked at him. Then he sprang at the sobbing, frightened boy, caught him and shook him, cuffing him hither and thither around the sail-room. Ti begged and protested, but blow followed blow.

At length Lum Lee forced him into a bowed posture before the idol. Lighting the incense sticks, the uncle placed them himself before Poo Saat. Then he struck Ti again and, leaving him, went away.

The idol Poo Saat looked on immovable. The fumes of the incense sticks filled the room. The twilight deepened into dark as the boy lay there sobbing under his breath. He crept away from the idol, and, sore and trembling, lay down on an old sail. Poo Saat could hardly be distinguished in the darkness that enveloped the room.

Ti felt very lonely. "I want the teacher woman!" he sobbed. "She told me, 'Little children, keep yourselves from idols.'"

He was afraid to leave the sail-room and go back to the tiny, crowded house where he lived with Uncle Lum Lee and his wife and children, and his aunt, the wife of the uncle who had gone to China. Ti knew that his other aunt, Lum Lee's wife, would not sympathize with him at all. It was only yesterday that he had heard her praying to the kitchen god, saying, "O kitchen god! I pray you preserve my two pigs, that this year they may grow fat and large, so as to be sold for a great many cash! And then I will come and worship you!" And even the other aunt with whom Ti had lived in the city, might tell him he had done wrong not to obey his Uncle Lum Lee.

The boy had had no supper and he did not know whether anybody had carried old See Yow any rice. He cried and sobbed over and over, "I want my Jesus teacher!"

He thought he had done right, but oh, it had been so hard! He wanted somebody to help him. The teacher woman would be sorry. She would tell him what to do if she were here. How could he live with his uncle and not worship idols, if he must be whipped this way? Did the Jesus book mean that a Chinese boy must never worship idols — never, though he was struck and whipped?

"I want my Jesus teacher!" wept Ti.

Then, as he sobbed on from sheer nervousness and pain, there came to the suffering child the thought that Jesus was here, if the teacher woman was not. He lifted his tear-stained face and looked toward the idol Poo Saat. The incense sticks had burned out. Ti gazed at the almost invisible idol, and the thought grew in him that Jesus was really here, and that he need not cry so very long and unhappily. Then he began to pray. He prayed in his own words, as the teacher had taught him, and the comfort that the little lonely boy needed came into his heart as he told Jesus everything.

The sail-room grew darker. The idol Poo Saat became invisible, and tired, bruised Ti fell asleep on the old sail.

By and by he woke. There was a soft step in the dark. A figure crept to his side.

"Eat!" whispered somebody, and he knew it was his aunt, Ah Cheng.

Ti ate his rice out of the little bowl in the dark. His aunt said she had fed See Yow, but the old man could eat almost nothing. He had seemed very happy, though, she said, but she did not know why.

Ti finished his rice, and his aunt crept silently away through the dark and left the tired boy to finish his night's sleep in the sail-room, guarded not by the idol Poo Saat, but by the One of whom the teacher had taught him.

In the gray of the early morning, while the fog yet rested heavily upon the bay, Ti came out of the sail-house and hurried to See Yow's shed. Early as it was, the old man lay awake upon his hard board covered with a piece of matting. In his great joy he had not slept much this night. He had found what his soul sought. He looked at his little friend and smiled as the boy came into the shed.

Ti came to the old man's side and sat down. He had come for comfort, but he was unprepared for the look of joy on See Yow's face.

"Jesus Christ has made the center of my heart understand the new words!" said the sick man in Chinese faintly but joyfully. "I am only an old fisherman Chinaman, but I know the new words! I never heard them when I was young. I have heard them when I am old, a very poor old fisherman Chinaman. Jesus loves me. I have come to him. The center of my heart is very glad."

There was such a look on his face as Ti had never seen there before. It made him think of the teacher woman in the city.

"The center of my heart understands the new words!" repeated See Yow faintly. "Jesus Christ loves me, Jesus Christ loves me — me, a very poor, old fisherman Chinaman!"

Ti had meant to tell his old friend of the blows Uncle Lum Lee had given and the harsh words he had spoken. He was sore from some of the blows still, but the wonder of seeing the joy on the sick man's face kept the boy from speaking of his own experiences. Suddenly he found the tears rolling down his face. He was so glad for See Yow.

"I am glad for you! I am glad!" sobbed he; and the old Chinaman put his hand on the boy's, and the two were silent for a time.

Ti could not tell what he felt. He knew that See Yow had become a "Jesus man." Oh, how glad, how happy a thing that was! The child did not say a word about his own troubles. He had almost forgotten for the moment that he had any, in the wonder and gladness of the thought that See Yow was a "Jesus man."

When it grew quite light, Ti went away to his uncle's hut. Lum Lee had already gone out in a boat with some other Chinamen, and his wife let Ti have some breakfast, though she spoke harshly to him, for she was a woman of violent temper. Ti carried See Yow some food, and then began work.

But never from that day did Lum Lee seem to like his nephew. He was cross and abusive to the boy, till, as months went by, he even wished that his other uncle might come back from China to take him away from the harsh words and blows. He was so willing a worker that Uncle Lum Lee could not complain of laziness, but he found all the fault he could in every other way.

Aunt Ah Cheng was very sorry. She shielded Ti all she was able, but she told him she wished he would worship the gods. Ah Cheng was really afraid not to worship certain gods herself. Under more favorable circumstances she might have been a Christian. But she had not had as much good teaching as Ti, and though he and she sometimes went to old See Yow's shed and talked a little of the "Jesus doctrine," yet she would afterwards assist Lum Lee's wife in worshiping the "kitchen god," and she still worshiped before her old picture of the goddess of mercy, Kun Yam.

Only a few of the Chinamen went to see See Yow while he was sick. To those who did come he spoke now of the "new words," but the Chinese looked at him and said he had an evil spirit. One day the old man died with the prayer on his lips, "Jesus Christ, make all the Chinese understand the new words."

Then one of the Chinamen who lived with others in the hut that See Yow had formerly occupied, went out in a panic and scraped down the old red paper that had been pasted there so long ago, the paper that contained the "new words." Generally Chinese look with respect on paper printed with Chinese characters, but this was different.

"It is a bad paper," said the other Chinamen. "It brings evil spirits! See what it did to See Yow!"

So the Chinaman scraped down every vestige of the paper, and the wind from the bay blew the small red fragments out of the narrow street into the fields outside the squalid little hamlet. But the red paper had done the work whereunto it was sent. One soul had come to know the reality of the "new words."

Down in the city the teacher women worked and prayed and wept and struggled against the heathenism of the great Chinese quarter. Sometimes it seemed to them as if their hearts would break over the wrong and the cruelty they saw. They wept that they could do no more. They never had seen See Yow. They had never even heard of him. They would not meet him now, till that day when he would come to them in heaven and say, " Your work reached even to me! You never saw me, but you taught a little Chinese boy, and he told me what the 'new words' meant. He told me about Jesus."

But, alas for Ti! As the months went by after old See Yow's death, and Uncle Lum Lee continued to be so harsh and to strike him so many times for not worshiping before the idols, the boy gradually almost ceased to pray to Jesus for help to be a true Christian. Whipped and unkindly treated, the little lad lost courage. At last he bowed before the idols, he put up the incense sticks, he burned paper money before the ancestral tablet. At first, when he did these things, a very unhappy feeling came into his heart, a sense of having grieved Jesus, and he went away and cried. His aunt, Ah Cheng, found it out, and she said to him: "If you and I lived alone you could worship Jesus Christ, I would not prevent it. But now we must live with Uncle Lum Lee, and it is foolish that you should let yourself be whipped. Worship the idols when he wishes. Then he will not strike you so much."

Alas! The boy listened to these words, and he did as Aunt Ah Cheng said. Not that he went and bowed before the idols of his own accord. He did not do that. But whenever Lum Lee said so, Ti went and burned incense before Poo Saat, or went through any other heathen rite of worship that his uncle wished.

So the months went on. Yet the boy was not happy, for at times a voice in his heart seemed to say, "Ti, dear Ti, Jesus loves you. Will you not be brave for love of him?"

Lum Lee was in the sail-room, before the idol Poo Saat, making trial of the Kà-pue. The Kà-pue, or wooden divining blocks, were in Lum Lee's hands. He was seeking, after Chinese method, to obtain from the idol some expression of its will in regard to a business project that he wanted to enter upon. A Chinaman from another California Chinese fishing-hamlet on a bay a great many miles down the coast, had offered to exchange his business interests there for Lum Lee's here.

Lum Lee was rather anxious to make the exchange. The bargain looked advantageous to him, and he believed that he would make more money at the other fishing-hamlet than he made where he now was. But he also believed in consulting the gods before entering upon any important business change, so yesterday he had consulted the idol by means of the wooden divining blocks, Kà-pue, and the blocks had most unfortunately fallen so that, according to Chinese interpretation, they meant an unfavorable answer.

"Don't you do it," was what Lum Lee thought the blocks said, and he did not like such an answer as that. He wanted the idol to approve of his new business plan, so he thought he would try the Kà-pue again. Perhaps the idol would consent.

The Kà-pue, or divining blocks, are from three to eight inches long, and each has a flat and a round side. If the two blocks, when thrown, fall with both round sides up, the answer is unfavorable. That was the way Kà-pue had fallen yesterday.

Kà-pue.
Fallen with the two curved sides uppermost, meaning unfavorable answer.

Lum Lee hoped they would not fall so now. He knelt, and bowed before the idol several times while kneeling. Then he once again stated his plans, and begged for an answer from the idol. Then he took the divining blocks and put their two flat surfaces together. With a circular motion he passed the blocks through the smoke of the burning incense a few times, then reverently threw them up before the idol, so that the two blocks would fall between the idol and himself.

The Kà-puc fell on the floor. Lum Lee looked. Oh, joy! They had not fallen as they did yesterday! Now, one block had fallen with its flat side up, and the other with its round side up! That meant

Kà-puc.
With one block flat side up, and the other round side up, meaning affirmative or favorable answer.

"yes!" The idol had consented! He could exchange his business with the other Chinaman.

Satisfied with this answer, and ignoring the opposite answer of yesterday, Lum Lee was not many days in completing the bargain with the Chinaman from the southern fishing-hamlet, who, in his turn, was persuaded that he could make money in Lum Lee's shrimp business.

The bargain being consummated, Lum Lee gathered his possessions and took his wife and children and Ti and Ah Cheng and sailed on the fishing-hamlet's junk to the city. Ah Cheng's husband had been gone to China for almost a year now. Privately, Lum Lee doubted whether he would ever return, since opium smoking and gambling were making such a wreck of him. He was probably going down lower and lower in China, and becoming more useless to himself and everybody else. But if he ever did return to America, he could almost as easily find his wife and Ti at one fishing-hamlet as at the other. Uncle Lum Lee wanted to take Ah Cheng and Ti with him, because he had proved their capacity for working, and he thought he would be richer with two extra pairs of hands to work for him. Ah Cheng and Ti had almost nothing to say about the moving.

The junk neared the city. It was the first time Ti had been there since his hurried departure that night almost a year ago, for he had not been allowed any city trips by his uncle, who wanted the boy to work diligently. He hoped that now Uncle Lum Lee would allow him to go up from the wharves to the Chinese quarter a little while, to try to find the teacher woman.

But Lum Lee allowed no such thing. He left his folks on board the junk, and went to get tickets for the rest of the voyage. For the fishing village to which he was transporting himself and his family was not isolated like the hamlet where they had been living. The new home was to be in a Chinese fishing-hamlet between two American towns on the southern bay, and steamboats and American sailing vessels went to and fro frequently between the city and one of the southern towns. So Uncle Lum Lee, who had known what day to come to the city, found no difficulty in buying tickets for his folks on a

TI: A STORY OF CHINATOWN. 79

sailing vessel that was going to start south that afternoon.

Leaving the junk to be taken back to the old Chinese village by the other allow his nephew to go abroad in the city streets.

The little party waited till sailing time, and the vessel moved away with them out

Chinese Wayside Stand — Shells for Sale.

Chinamen who had accompanied the moving family down, Ti and Ah Cheng and Uncle Lum Lee and his folks and his household possessions formed a hasty, almost unobserved little procession across to another wharf where was the sailing vessel. Once on board that, Lum Lee would not through the Golden Gate to the blue Pacific. After considerable sailing, they came at last to the bay they sought, and across its blue water Ti could see a long wharf reaching out from an American town. At the wharf the ship stopped. There were queer old Mexican buildings in the town, and there were American and Spanish and Chinese faces. Beyond the town, stretching toward the direction they were to go, Ti could see a great many pine trees. Uncle Lum Lee hired a Chinese laundry wagon to transport his possessions to the Chinese village, and the whole party rode with the things.

Ti felt homesick. He did not know anything about the new home to which he was going, but he looked at Aunt Ah Cheng's sad face, and he knew that Uncle Lum Lee would be as harsh and exacting in the new home as in the old.

He looked out at the tall pines, as the wagon passed on, and he heard blue-jays scream from the tree tops. There were American wagons on the road, coming and going, for the two American bay towns were only a couple of miles apart, and houses straggled along the way. The farther town was a great resort for summer visitors, and the Chinaman who was driving told Lum Lee that many of those American visitors bought sea shells of the Chinese. On one road the Chinese had a wayside stand for selling shells to the tourists who were at this season riding hither and thither. Many of the Americans — some of whom were visitors from Eastern States — frequently walked over the fields, by the path near the rocky shore, to the Chinese hamlet and purchased shells there. These visitors often admired the abalone shells, and bought "sets" of them of different sizes. Also there was the trade of going around selling fish to the many Americans who had homes in the two towns between which the Chinese hamlet was situated.

All this did the laundry wagon Chinaman, as he drove, tell to Uncle Lum Lee and his folks. Lum Lee's avaricious eyes glittered with satisfaction. Surely he would make much money in this place. How foolish that other Chinaman had been to exchange business with him! How much better living in this place would be than living away from all money-possessing Americans at the shrimp-curing hamlet, as he had heretofore done! How well that the divining blocks fell propitiously for the plan of moving! Ah, Lum Lee did not realize that there is One mightier than idols. Little did he dream what this removal was to mean for Ti.

CHAPTER XIII.

AH CHENG CHOOSES.

OWN toward the rocks beside the bay, Ti could see the great waves come splashing high, white with foam, and there was a fresh wind. The wagon turned from the road and went down a lane and across a field, and there, on the edge of the blue bay, was the Chinese fishing-hamlet. Fish were drying on rough wooden tables back of the hamlet. There was a jargon of Chinese voices. Chinese boats were beached on the sandy

shore next the rocks. Two tables of different kinds of shells, mainly great abalone shells with their beautiful, iridescent interiors, and strings of various sized sea-urchin shells, stood beside the street. One stand had the English sign, "Shell for Sale," evidently written by some Chinaman.

Across the fields, beyond the Chinese hamlet, not a very long distance, began the other American town, among the pines. It had originally been only a camping place, but now it had grown to be a town with streets and churches and business houses and a hotel. Many people had built houses and lived here the year around, although there were still many rows of wooden-framed, canvas-covered tents among the pines for those people who preferred to live in tents instead of houses. American artists, ladies and gentlemen, often came over from the settlement and sat sketching the Chinese houses and boats and children.

Ti saw one Chinaman who had just come in from making a tour, hunting abalone shells around some of the coasts of this peninsula. The Chinaman carried an iron rod to knock abalones off the rocks, and he told Ti he had been away around by the light-house, at a certain

There were rows of tents.

The Light-house.

point situated far beyond where the boy had yet seen.

Lum Lee hurried his family to the house in the loft of which they were to live. The house was a very small one, and the loft consisted of only two little rooms, but into them were crowded the household belongings, the god shelf was set up, and, leaving Ti and Ah Cheng and his wife and children there, Uncle Lum Lee went away to attend to his business interests.

The houses of the hamlet were all small, forming the crowded homes of many Chinese. The fields spread widely along the shore. There was room there, but the houses were all huddled together, according to Chinese ideas of crowding.

Ti soon found that this was a busy place for him. Almost everybody was busy. Young Chinese girls carried on their backs little baby brothers or sisters, while attending to the fish, and the women went out in boats to gather kelp. Some of the numerous children of the village were already beginning to be traders in shells with the American visitors, and demanded "fi' cent" for a string of small sea-urchin shells.

Ti was needed for various things — to

The Chinese Fishing Hamlet.

go fishing with Uncle Lum Lee and the other men, to go over to the American settlement among the pines, selling fish. Moreover, he had to learn to go with iron rod, searching along the seashore rocks for miles, hunting for abalones. Some afternoons he spent sifting the white beach sand through his fingers, hunting for the tiny "rice shells" that look like grains of rice and can be sold to Americans. Above all, he must attend to the fish-drying and the turning of the multitudes of tiny fish on the rocks and drying tables. Moreover, he could gather pine cones in the woods, and sell sacks of them to the campers for fuel. All these ways of earning money

TI: A STORY OF CHINATOWN.

for Uncle Lum Lee were shown Ti during the first few days here.

The first Sunday came, and with it a piece of news that startled Ti. After a person had gone by the village shrine, and had passed along the crooked street by the houses, and had turned to the right, there stood a house the use of which the boy had never thought to inquire, during the few days he had lived here. On Sunday, however, two women came through the village. Ti supposed they were Americans who had perhaps come to see the hamlet, or to buy shells, for he knew that all Americans did not refrain from buying things on Sunday. Presently he noticed that the two women were stopping here and there at the houses, gathering little Chinese children.

"Where you go?" asked Ti of one little Chinese boy, Hip Lon.

"Go to Jesus teacher women's school to-day," said Hip Lon. "You go?"

Astonished Ti could hardly believe it true. Could it be possible that there were Jesus teacher women here in this Chinese fishing-hamlet? He questioned Hip Lon and discovered that these were indeed Jesus teachers, and that they lived in a house up among the pines over the hill, and that they always came down to the fishing-hamlet Sundays and held a little Sunday-school for the Chinese children in the house near the edge of the hamlet, the house of which he had not thought to inquire the use.

"Oh, I go once to Chinese Jesus teachers' school up in the city!" exclaimed surprised, excited Ti to Hip Lon, and then he ran to find Aunt Ah Cheng, and beg her to let him go to the teacher women's school. Little Hip Lon looked after Ti, as he ran away to find his aunt,

Hip Lon's small sister.

astonished that he should be so excited over the news of the school.

Aunt Ah Cheng consented to Ti's excited appeal, though she knew Uncle Lum Lee would be angry if he discovered it.

So Ti went with Hip Lon and his small sister. Neither of these teachers was the loved teacher from the city, of course, but they noticed Ti immediately when he came to school. They noticed that he knew one of the songs sung there, and by questioning him found that he had once been a mission scholar in the city.

Thus began Ti's acquaintance with the teachers. Much surprised were they to discover that he had a "Jesus book" and that he remembered many Bible texts he had learned in the city. But there was one thing the teachers could not know, and that was how, now, in the hamlet Sunday-school, the songs about Christ and the teachers' words smote the boy's heart. How he had meant once to be true to Jesus, and how sadly he felt he had failed! How many times he had bowed to idols! How there came back to Ti now words that his dear, kind city teacher had said to him! "How good she was to me!" he thought repentantly, "and how grieved she would be if she knew that I bowed to idols and burned incense to them!"

Sunday after Sunday, as Ti slipped into the hamlet Sunday-school, the struggle in his heart grew. Sometimes his uncle would not let him go to the school. He would not have allowed the boy to go at all, if it had not been that during the week the teachers sometimes bought fish of Lum Lee. Then he would, the next Sunday, scowlingly permit Ti to go to Sunday-school, for fear of offending a fish-customer.

But whether Ti went to Sunday-school or not, the voice that spoke to the boy's heart would be heard, and he was unhappy. Ah, how unhappy is a heart that has loved Jesus and then wanders away from him! Ti knew that if he began again to refuse to worship idols he would be whipped and cuffed and cursed by Uncle Lum Lee and his wife, as before. He dreaded meeting such treatment again. So, daily, he dissembled. But, oh, how unhappy he felt when certain songs were sung in the teachers' school! How he had to struggle to keep the tears back! It almost seemed as if he could hear his loved city teacher say, "Oh, Ti, I want you to love Jesus while you are a little boy!" Ah, the good Shepherd was calling his little lamb! Wandering Ti was not forgotten.

So surprised and interested were the teachers in discovering that Ti had once been a mission pupil in the city, that they found out from him the name of his teacher there. Then, after some writing hither and thither, the teachers of the hamlet found out the address of his former city teacher.

One evening, one of the hamlet teachers sent word to Ti asking him to come up to their house over the hill among the pines. The boy thought that perhaps some fish was wanted, or the teachers needed some errand done. So he went to their house. He was very greatly surprised to find that one of them had a letter from his former teacher in the city. The hamlet teacher, on discovering her address, had written and told her they had found one of her former pupils.

Ah, how glad a letter did the city teacher send back! She had thought that

Ti was in China, since she had seen his uncle going on the China steamer. She had pictured the boy surrounded by heathenism. And now to find that he was still in this country, and that he had been guided to a hamlet where there were other Christian workers to teach him! Ah, surely God's hand was in Lum Lee's moving to this place.

"Tell Ti," wrote the city teacher, "how very glad I am to hear of him! Tell him I have prayed for him every day since he went away. Tell him to be sure to keep on praying to Jesus. He will help him if he asks him." And then the letter closed with these words: "Dear Ti, do try to be a real Christian!"

Ti listened intently as the teacher read. But there was a look on his face that she did not understand. The boy was silent a moment after the letter was finished. The tears began to roll down his face. Suddenly the remorse that had overwhelmed him as he heard the loving words, grew too strong for concealment. He dropped, sobbing, on his knees at the teacher's feet.

"I used to love Jesus in the city," he sobbed. "Now I am bad boy so long. Jesus will never love me again."

Sobbing, he told his story — how he had gone from the city to the other fishing-hamlet to live, how he had been beaten by Uncle Lum Lee for not worshiping Poo Saat, how at last he had yielded and now for many months had worshiped Chinese idols.

"Jesus will never love me again, I am bad boy so long!" wept Ti over and over. "Oh, I am bad! I am bad!"

The tears came into the teacher's eyes. She knew how very hard it often is for Chinese to become Christians, since they must meet with so much reviling and perhaps cruelty from relatives.

"Ti," she said as she bent over the sobbing boy beside her, "Ti, Jesus does forgive you. He loves you. He is sorry for you and is sorry to have you worship idols, for they can do you no good. But he wants you to know that he still loves you, and will help you to be brave if you turn to him."

Long and tenderly the teacher talked with the repentant boy. She prayed with him, and Ti prayed for himself. It was broken prayer, but it came from a heart repentant as Peter's for his denial. And when Ti went away homeward toward the Chinese fishing-hamlet he was happy in the thought that Jesus loved him, and the knowledge of this great love made him feel strong. He looked up at the evening sky and said, not as he so often had, "I am bad boy so long Jesus never love me again," but instead, "Dear Jesus, I don't care what happens, I will never worship idols again, for I know you love me and will help me."

It did not take Lum Lee and his wife long to perceive the change in Ti. He neither worshiped the gods nor offered mock paper money before his father's tablet. Uncle Lum Lee struck the little boy, and his wife reviled him as one most despised by the Chinese — a son who is ungrateful to his dead father. "You have burned no paper money before your father's tablet for two weeks!" she said angrily one day. "Your father's spirit is poor! How can he have any money when you do not burn it? His spirit is poor! He is hungry! But you do not care! You are wicked! You do not care for your father now he is dead!"

Ti did not answer. Once, such an accusation would almost have broken his heart, for he still loved and missed his father.

His aunt struck him some half dozen sharp blows on the side of his head, and passed on, her face lowering. How could she know that the boy, his face smarting from the blows, was praying silently for help?

Many days were very hard for Ti, now. Lum Lee's wife told the other Chinese about him, and they treated him severely. Hip Lon's mother said sternly in Chinese to him, "Once when I was in China, my father went to the house of a high mandarin. When my father came back, he told us children what he had seen there. He saw a picture of an old woman. It meant the mandarin's grandmother. Always, night and day, the mandarin had large red candles burning before the picture. Also he burned incense. His sons and daughters came and knocked heads to the picture. You are poor, and you cannot offer great red candles always to your father, but you can burn paper money for him! You are a bad son to illtreat your father when he is dead!"

Ti listened, but he did not answer. Yet sometimes, when the days were very hard, and he was tired with much work, and Lum Lee struck him and reviled him as a "Jesus boy," Ti hid himself in the field and cried. But he prayed, too.

The teachers guessed how it was with their little pupil. They said a comforting, strengthening word to him when they met him during the week. Uncle Lum Lee would not let him go to the Sunday-school any more, even if the teachers did not buy fish of him. Therefore it was many weeks before Ti knew something that was coming to pass. It was this:

His aunt, Ah Cheng, watched the boy very closely now. She knew his troubles, though she said nothing. Living in the same crowded loft with Lum Lee's folks, Ah Cheng saw that Ti would rather be struck than worship the gods. Sometimes she guessed that he prayed in the night secretly to the "true God." She disliked to have the little lad struck and abused so much by Lum Lee and his wife, and as she watched him through the months, his influence over her deepened. Not that he was a perfect Christian. He was far from that. There were days when he felt impatient and did wrong, but Ah Cheng could see that he tried to do right.

Long ago, when Ti had been faithful and had borne blows for Jesus' sake, Ah

Cheng was touched. If he had remained faithful she might have been different now. As it was, his conduct began to have great influence over her.

One Sunday afternoon the teachers were surprised to see Ah Cheng slip into their Sunday-school and sit at one side, listening. Ti was not there, and his aunt seemed afraid that it would be known she had come, for she glanced apprehensively toward the door now and then. She soon slipped out, but after that she came every Sunday for a few minutes. Gradually she stayed longer.

Ah Cheng never said anything about why she came or what she heard there. She only sat and listened with the children. Sometimes there was so longing a look in her eyes that the teachers wanted to speak to her, but she seemed to wish to avoid notice, and they were afraid of causing her to stay away, if they said anything to her. So she slipped quietly in and out, and when she was there the only notice the teachers took of her presence was to have the little ones repeat after them the plainest and simplest truths in their lesson, carefully explaining themselves, as the lesson went on. For the teachers knew that the Chinese woman needed to have the truth presented to her as plainly as to a little child, and that the things the children spoke or sang might reach her heart when their own words would not. But the teachers were not quite prepared for what followed.

One day, when all the Chinese fisher people were busy, off fishing, or drying fish outside the hamlet, or doing the same thing on the beach, or attending to the many tasks always necessary, Aunt Ah Cheng went swiftly up to the loft where she and Lum Lee's folks lived. Nobody was there. She had thought nobody would be there this time of day. Lum Lee's wife was off turning fish on the rocks.

There was a strange look on Ah Cheng's face. Her hands were trembling. She took down her long-worshiped picture of the goddess of mercy, Kun Yam. Hurrying, trembling, she gathered whatever she owned that pertained to idol-worship — the incense sticks, the mock paper money — but she did not touch anything that belonged to Lum Lee's god shelf or idol-worship.

Hiding in her dress these various things of her own, with the picture of the goddess of mercy, Ah Cheng went tremblingly down the outside stairs to a near-by shed. This shed, almost next to Lum Lee's home, was used by a number of families as a cooking place. There was a sort of open fireplace, and in this, now, were some hot coals, for it was not long since eating time.

No one beside Ah Cheng was in the shed. Hastily she stirred the live coals, and laid on them the old picture of the goddess of mercy. The picture flamed up in an instant. Ah Cheng laid the other things in the flames. She waited, trembling all over. She hid her face.

No one came. When she looked up, the picture of Kun Yam, before whom Ah Cheng had been used to worship, was reduced to ashes. There was no trace of the other things save a few ends of incense sticks, and these Ah Cheng pushed further on the coals. A slight blaze rose, and the last trace of the things of which she had made the fire was gone. Only the live coals waited, glowing still.

Ah Cheng covered the coals with ashes. She rose and caught hold of the doorway to steady herself. Then she went away again to the fish-curing.

The evening of that day, when Ti came home to the loft, he found uproar there. Lum Lee's wife was full of fury.

"Will you be a Jesus doctrine woman?" she screamed at Ah Cheng.

"Yes," said Ah Cheng, quietly but firmly.

Then Lum Lee's wife burst into a storm of Chinese reviling. And when a furious Chinese woman reviles, she can do it with the turbulence of a torrent.

But it was useless. Ah Cheng had chosen. She was ignorant of many things, but she had chosen Christ. It was not a lightly made resolve. She had known what the consequences would be. For a long time she had been silently watching, thinking, wavering. Now she had burned her gods, and she stood firmly. She had found peace in Christ. There was no great, overwhelming emotion in Ah Cheng's case, but she had trust and rest and peace in her heart, for Jesus was with her. She had weighed the matter carefully, and deliberately she had taken Christ for her Helper, though she knew the choice involved persecution.

CHAPTER XIV.

"GOD BLESS YOU, TI."

LUM LEE'S wife was fairly beside herself with rage. She drove Ti and Ah Cheng out of the house that night, declaring that Christians who burned the gods should not stay under the same roof with her.

As all the other little houses of the hamlet were crowded, Ah Cheng and Ti were forced to sleep that night under some empty fish-drying tables at one side of the hamlet. The next day, however, Lum Lee's wife permitted them to come back to the loft to live. Lum Lee knew they were good workers, and he did not want them to stray from the hamlet back to the city.

But his wife continued her vituperations, and made the succeeding days as uncomfortable as she could. All the Chinese in the hamlet heard from her what Ah Cheng had done in burning the picture of the goddess of mercy. Some of the more superstitious women regarded the act with horror, for though the teachers of the Mission school had tried to do what they could in instructing the Chinese people of the hamlet about Christianity, yet the main influence of the instruction had been on the little Chinese children. Only here and there was one among the women or the men who might possibly be silently thinking and weighing the subject, even as Ah Cheng had done, but who lacked courage to come out openly in favor of the "Jesus doctrine."

Several of the more superstitious women of the hamlet openly prophesied that some evil spirit would do harm to Ah Cheng. But the weeks passed, and no harm came. Ah Cheng labored faithfully at the fish-curing, and finally Lum Lee's wife settled into a sullen acceptance of the fact of her Christianity. The home loft was a very uncomfortable place, though, usually, for Ah Cheng and Ti. Two believers in the "Jesus doctrine" were a constant invitation, Lum Lee's wife believed, to evil spirits to enter the loft and do harm. Yet there were so many Chinese in this hamlet, in comparison to the small number of houses, that every house was crowded, Chinese fashion, and there was no other place for the two to stay, had any other family felt disposed to offer them a home.

Some five or six months of this uncomfortable manner of living went by. Ti and Ah Cheng tried to be faithful. So long a time had elapsed that the neighbors had ceased to say evil would come because of the burning of the goddess of mercy's picture. Other things engaged the neighbors' attention, though many of the people did not favor the Jesus doctrine.

One night, about eleven o'clock, when the Chinese hamlet was still, Ti was awakened by a loud crackling sound and a sense of suffocation. The loft was full of dense smoke. He heard his Aunt Ah Cheng crying to him, "Ti! Ti!"

There were cries of frightened people in the street below. Half a dozen of the little Chinese houses were on fire.

"Ti!" screamed Ah Cheng in Chinese. "Hurry! Hurry!"

Lum Lee's wife was shrieking. She snatched up one of her children. Ti caught up the youngest child.

"Quick! Quick!" screamed Ah Cheng.

Struggling through the strangling smoke, they pushed their way out the door to the stairway. The steps leading down to the street were on fire! The street was full of running, screaming, frightened Chinese women and men, who did not know what to do. Ti and Ah Cheng and Lum Lee's folks climbed over the already burning roof of their loft. They dropped to the upper outside top of a flight of steps of another house that was also on fire, and escaped to the street.

Running across the fields came American men, rushing to help. "Chinatown's afire!" they shouted to one another. Into the midst of the wailing, shrieking Chinese women ran the white helpers. White men darted here and there, helped by some Chinese, finding old boilers, empty oil cans, old buckets. Men ran to the beach for sea-water. The air was full of cinders. White men and Chinamen climbed here and there, throwing the water over roofs and walls. The fire had probably caught from the cook shed near Uncle Lum Lee's house, the shed in which several families were wont to cook, and where some one probably had carelessly left too much fire early in the evening.

On the edge of the hamlet, some American women and small boys who had run down from the nearest houses of the town among the pines, stood and watched the fire. For a little time, it looked as though a good part of the hamlet of dry, tinder-like houses would be swept away, but the sea-water and the exertions of the workers prevailed against the flames at last. They died down. Only half a dozen of the little houses had been consumed.

"It's a good thing none of you lost your lives!" said one of the white men cheerfully to the crowd of frightened Chinese. "The fire must have started from that cook shed you say was here, and burned each way, taking houses on both sides. Somebody left live coals uncovered last night, and there was a wind, you know."

Now, among the company of frightened women was one who, from murmurs of other Chinese, caught the white man's meaning, and she knew that she had probably been the last person who cooked in the shed the previous evening. Consequently she knew she was very likely the one who had been careless about leaving the fire so that it had crept to the dry, wooden side of the rickety shed. The woman did not know whether anybody knew she had been the last person in the cook shed. She was very much afraid of being accused of being guilty for the fire, for some of the Chinese who had had their household goods burned were in an angry mood.

But, in her fright, this woman suddenly thought of something. If only she could make Lum Lee's wife think that this fire had come as a punishment for Ah Cheng's having burned the goddess of mercy's picture! Then suspicion might be turned away from herself, if anybody had begun to try to remember who had cooked last in the shed.

The woman edged her way to Lum Lee's wife and said something. In an instant the latter's superstitious fears were aroused, angry as she was over the loss of household things. The fire indeed must have come from the insulted goddess of mercy! Had not Ah Cheng burned her picture?

With a cry of hatred, Lum Lee's wife rushed toward Ah Cheng.

"The curse of Kun Yam made the fire come!" she screamed in Chinese. "It is the curse of the goddess of mercy! Ah Cheng burned the picture of Kun Yam in the fire! Now Kun Yam has sent the fire to burn Ah Cheng, and it has burned all our things, too! Ah Cheng is a Jesus believer! Ah Cheng brought the fire on us!"

With clenched fist the excited woman struck at Ah Cheng, who put up both hands to ward off the blow.

"I was not in the cook shed at all last evening," protested frightened Ah Cheng in Chinèse. "I did not have a fire there!"

But it was useless to protest, for Lum Lee's wife did not listen. She had not ceased to scream, "It is the curse of Kun Yam! Ah Cheng is a Jesus doctrine woman! She makes Kun Yam send fire to burn us! She burned Kun Yam's picture in the fire, and Kun Yam sends fire back on us!"

The cry of Lum Lee's wife found an answer in some of the more superstitious hearts of her ignorant Chinese neighbors whose houses had been burned. These neighbors began to mutter angrily. Ti stood by his aunt, who vainly protested again that she had not been in the cook shed the previous evening.

"Ah Cheng brings fire on us!" screamed Lum Lee's wife.

"What is all this trouble?" asked the stern voice of an American man, who did not understand Chinese.

Ah Cheng was trembling. The neighbors were beginning to look angrily at her, as they continued muttering among themselves. But a quick form slipped through the crowd.

"Ah Cheng," said one of the teachers quietly, "you and Ti come home with me to-night. This hamlet was so crowded, before, that now, with half a dozen houses burned, there will hardly be room for all to sleep. You and Ti come with me."

The teacher hurried Ah Cheng and Ti away from the hamlet. The fire being over, American people were returning homeward across the fields.

"Don't cry, Ah Cheng," said the teacher kindly in broken Chinese and English, as she heard a stifled sob from the poor frightened creature while they hastened on across the fields towards the teachers' house over the hill among the pines. "It was not your fault that the fire came. You had not been in the shed. Kun Yam did not send the fire, either. Some other Chinese woman was careless. Make your aunt understand what I say, Ti. You can talk better Chinese than I can. She's too frightened just now to understand much English."

So Ti repeated to his aunt in Chinese what the teacher had said.

"Oh, Jesus teacher woman!" sobbed Ah Cheng in Chinese, "Chinese all hate me now! All say I make the goddess of mercy send fire, because I burn Kun Yam! All Chinese hate me now! But I had to burn Kun Yam's picture, because Jesus book tells me not to pray to make-believe gods any more. Now Chinese all hate me! Ti and I have no home any more!"

The teacher's heart was full of loving sympathy. She remembered One who had not where to lay his head. She remembered the words, "Blessed are ye, when men shall revile you, and persecute you, and shall say all manner of evil against you falsely, for my sake."

"Ah Cheng," she said gently, "do not be afraid. Jesus will take care of you. I do not think all the Chinese will hate you. It is only Lum Lee's wife who tries to make the other women think the fire came from the idol's anger."

But in her heart the teacher said, "I hope Ah Cheng will not have to go back to live with Lum Lee's wife any more and be struck and reviled! It is not as if this were a Chinese fishing-hamlet away on the coast, far from any American Christians. Here I can find work for her in some white Christian family."

The teacher knew that in the American town among the pines there were many comfortable Christian American families who lived there all the year around, and in some of them she was sure she could find a place where Ah Cheng might earn her living by washing and ironing, and another place where Ti could work, and they would be encouraged to keep on believing in Jesus and being true to him.

So the two stayed at the teachers' house that night. The next day, the teacher saw Uncle Lum Lee, who sullenly said he did not want Ah Cheng and Ti to come back and live with his family. He would have been glad to have their work, but his wife had declared she would not have Christians in the house again, lest they should bring more trouble on her from the goddess of mercy. His wife's talk had roused Lum Lee's superstitious fears, too, lest the gods should not prosper his money-getting.

"Clistians make Chinese joss mad!" said he angrily. "Joss send fire! No want Clistians! Make me lose money, if joss get mad!"

The teachers were thankful at heart that Lum Lee did not want Ah Cheng and Ti around any more. Being fearful, however, that he might change his mind after his superstitious fears had subsided, they thought best not to let Ah Cheng and Ti find places to work among the American Christians of the town among the pines, after all.

"It will be better for them at some Christian mission house in the city," decided the teachers, and they speedily wrote up to Ti's former city-mission teacher, asking her to come and take Ti and his aunt back with her to some Christian mission house for Chinese in the city.

The city teacher came speedily. Quickly were arrangements made, and one day Ti and Ah Cheng bade good-by to the kind teachers of the hamlet, and went with the city-mission teacher on board a vessel that was about to sail from the southern bay north toward the city once more.

The city teacher was thankful, as she stood beside Ti on the vessel after it had set sail, and knew that now the boy and his aunt would have a Christian home where they would no longer be struck and reviled and threatened because they did

TI: A STORY OF CHINATOWN. 93

not worship the gods. Ti could study and work. A Christian Chinese shoemaker had promised to teach him shoemaking in the city.

The teacher looked down at the boyish face beside her.

"Are you not glad to go back to the city, Ti?" she said.

The boy looked up with a quick smile. "Yes," he said, "I velly glad!"

Then he looked far across the water again, and the gladness faded from his face. The teacher looked where his gaze seemed fixed. She saw, far across the blue bay, the two American towns, and there between them a dark line on the bay shore. The line was the Chinese hamlet.

"What is it, Ti?" she asked, seeing the soberness of the child's gaze.

A wave of emotion swept over Ti's face. "Teacher," he said earnestly, his voice trembling with feeling, "I got two little Chinese cousin in that place, Lum Lee's little boy and girl. I 'fraid they never love Jesus! Teacher, I think of the other Chinese fishing place where I did live. Nobody there tell Chinese 'bout Jesus! Nobody came, all the time I live there, to tell Chinese 'bout Jesus! Teacher, great many little Chinese boys and girls in all Cal'forn'a! They don't know 'bout Jesus! Nobody teach them! Oh, teacher, it makes me feel bad! They don't know 'bout Jesus! Teacher, some day when I grow big, I go everywhere! I go tell all little Chinese girls and boys 'bout Jesus! Oh, teacher, I so glad you teach me 'bout Jesus when I was little!"

The boy choked. A great tear rolled down his cheek.

The teacher's own eyes were full. Too well did she know the stories of many of the hapless little ones who "don't know 'bout Jesus."

"God bless you, Ti," said she gently. "Tell them! Tell all the poor little Chinese children you can about Jesus. There are so few to tell them!"

Ti went away, and the teacher stood and looked afar across the water. She thought of the multitude of little Chinese children born and brought up in Christian America, and yet without Christian teaching. "They ought to be reached. They ought to be taught," she said to herself. "The poor little Chinese children! Often the parents won't believe us teachers when we tell them of Jesus and his love, but sometimes they will believe their children when they carry home the gospel we have taught them. Oh, if only there were more teachers to tell the story to the poor little Chinese children! Dear Lord, send forth more laborers into this, thine harvest!"

THE END.

www.ingramcontent.com/pod-product-compliance
Lightning Source LLC
Chambersburg PA
CBHW032247080426
42735CB00008B/1035